Ross Calvin

Ross Calvin
Interpreter of the American Southwest

Ron Hamm

SUNSTONE PRESS
SANTA FE

© 2016 by Ron Hamm
All Rights Reserved.
No part of this book may be reproduced in any form or by any electronic or mechanical means including information storage and retrieval systems without permission in writing from the publisher, except by a reviewer who may quote brief passages in a review.

Sunstone books may be purchased for educational, business, or sales promotional use. For information please write: Special Markets Department, Sunstone Press, P.O. Box 2321, Santa Fe, New Mexico 87504-2321.

Book and cover design › Vicki Ahl
Body typeface › Minion Pro
Printed on acid-free paper
∞
eBook 978-1-61139-456-6

Library of Congress Cataloging-in-Publication Data

Names: Hamm, Ron, 1935-
Title: Ross Calvin : interpreter of the American Southwest / by Ron Hamm.
Description: Santa Fe : Sunstone Press, 2016. | Includes bibliographical references.
Identifiers: LCCN 2016001665 (print) | LCCN 2016004156 (ebook) | ISBN 9781632931146 (hardcover : alkaline paper) | ISBN 9781632931153 (softcover : alkaline paper) | ISBN 9781611394566
Subjects: LCSH: Calvin, Ross, 1889-1970. | Calvin, Ross, 1889-1970--Travel--Southwest, New. | New Mexico--Biography. | Authors, American--New Mexico--Biography. | Calvin, Ross, 1889-1970. Sky determines. | New Mexico--In literature. | New Mexico--Description and travel. | Southwest, New--Description and travel. | Episcopal Church--New Mexico--Silver City--Clergy--Biography. | Silver City (N.M.)--Biography.
Classification: LCC F801.C28 H36 2016 (print) | LCC F801.C28 (ebook) | DDC 813/.4--dc23
LC record available at http://lccn.loc.gov/2016001665

SUNSTONE PRESS IS COMMITTED TO MINIMIZING OUR ENVIRONMENTAL IMPACT ON THE PLANET. THE PAPER USED IN THIS BOOK IS FROM RESPONSIBLY MANAGED FORESTS. OUR PRINTER HAS RECEIVED CHAIN OF CUSTODY (COC) CERTIFICATION FROM: THE FOREST STEWARDSHIP COUNCIL™ (FSC®), PROGRAMME FOR THE ENDORSEMENT OF FOREST CERTIFICATION™ (PEFC™), AND THE SUSTAINABLE FORESTRY INITIATIVE® (SFI®). THE FSC® COUNCIL IS A NON-PROFIT ORGANIZATION, PROMOTING THE ENVIRONMENTALLY APPROPRIATE, SOCIALLY BENEFICIAL AND ECONOMICALLY VIABLE MANAGEMENT OF THE WORLD'S FORESTS. FSC® CERTIFICATION IS RECOGNIZED INTERNATIONALLY AS A RIGOROUS ENVIRONMENTAL AND SOCIAL STANDARD FOR RESPONSIBLE FOREST MANAGEMENT.

WWW.SUNSTONEPRESS.COM
SUNSTONE PRESS / POST OFFICE BOX 2321 / SANTA FE, NM 87504-2321 /USA
(505) 988-4418 / ORDERS ONLY (800) 243-5644 / FAX (505) 988-1025

To my wife, Peggy, always in my corner.

Perhaps nowhere in the world is the natural setting nobler than in New Mexico—more beautiful with spacious desert, sky, mountain; more varied in rich, energizing climate, more dramatic in its human procession, more mellow with age-old charm. Endowed with sunshine that stimulates, and winter chill that toughens; with silence, vastness and majestic desert color that offer a spiritual companionship, it has enough. Here if anywhere is air, sky, earth fit to constitute a gracious homeland, not alone for those who occupy themselves in the world's work, but as well for those who study and create, for those who play, those who sit still to brood and dream.
—Ross Calvin, *Sky Determines* (1934)

Fear of dust in my mouth is always with me,
And I am the faithful husband of the rain

I am a dry man whose thirst is praise
Of clouds, and whose mind is something of a cup.

—Wendell Berry, "Water" (1970)

Contents

Introduction _____ 11

1. Learning Beckons _____ 15
2. A Love Lost, A New Family Begun _____ 28
3. Leaving "the Known World": The Silver City Years _____ 41
4. *Sky Determines* _____ 55
5. The Book's Reception _____ 64
6. The Book's Continuing Importance _____ 70
7. Lawrence Clark Powell: A Special Bond ____ 77
8. Church Tensions _____ 81
9. To the Plains: The Clovis Years _____ 93
10. *River of the Sun*: The Gila _____ 103
11. Later Publications _____ 111
12. Family Matters _____ 119
13. Cultivating His Garden _____ 125

Descendants of Ross Randall Calvin _____ 136
Notes and Sources _____ 141

Introduction

For reasons difficult to understand, neither the name Ross Calvin nor that of his principal work, the highlight of his career, is well known today, sadly not even in his adopted state. Yet *Sky Determines* (1934) occupies a unique niche in the pantheon of New Mexico nonfiction for its environmental and cultural interpretation of the Southwest. It was the first book about New Mexico I bought upon arriving here more than half a lifetime ago, and I find it continues to influence my understanding of the place I call home. Literary merits aside, a professional meteorologist who knows the book's premise well believes it is as valid today as it was when it was articulated eighty years ago. There have been and continue to be extreme weather events: sky still determines.

Calvin (1889–1970) deserves better than relative obscurity. His other major book, *River of the Sun* (1946), also should be dusted off and reread for its insights on the Gila River, which provide both a partial backdrop for the first book and a context for political machinations today. Calvin's premise in *Sky Determines* is that the Southwestern climate influences literally everything man does in this lovely but sometimes hostile setting—what he plants, what he eats, what he wears, where he shelters, whom or what he worships, and above all, when and where he drinks. At the end of the day, it may be nigh impossible to quantify just how much the sky matters. *Sky Determines* is not exactly the sort of book one would expect from an Episcopalian priest trained in English literature and philology at Harvard.

Sky Determines was received enthusiastically by critics and the reading public alike, both here and abroad. Reviewers said the book articulated a fresh new interpretation of an old thesis. Calvin introduced his readers to determinism, positing it against the dramatic backdrop of the Southwest—the idea that events are ultimately determined by causes outside the human will, e.g., for New Mexico, the climate. Geographic or climatic determinism became Calvin's "unrelenting theme," as one observer put it. At the time the book also resonated with Depression era readers eager for something, anything, to distract them from constant distressing economic news and with those who wanted to learn something about a part of the United States most did not know. Calvin must have been pleased when *The Nation* noted that his book was "poetically conceived and scientifically grounded"—"far from being a dull treatise." This was one of his first son's favorite quotes from reviews of his father's books.

External factors such as global warming may influence whether *Sky Determines* finds a new audience. Readers will find that the book will further their understanding and appreciation of the beauty of this magical land. One of Calvin's essays is titled "Looking Toward the Future." That is exactly what *Sky Determines* does. The companion publication of a facsimile edition by Sunstone Press is evidence that I am not alone in feeling that the book merits wider readership today.

While *Sky Determines* and *River of the Sun* were Calvin's major works, he also was asked to contribute a description of the people of New Mexico for the University of New Mexico's Department of Government publication *The Population of New Mexico*, 1947. More importantly, he provided an introduction and the notes to the 1951 reprint of *Lieutenant Emory Reports*, an undertaking that called again upon his scientific and literary training. The book describes the 1846–1847 march to the Pacific by General Stephen Kearney's Army of the West to determine if the Southwest was worth this country's effort to wrest it from Mexico. The account by young soldier-scientist Lieutenant William H. Emory made clear it was. As Emory put it, "We were not on an exploring expedition, war was the object." The young lieutenant's map-making skills were central to the effort. They were considered "so superb" and so accurate that they often made earlier maps obsolete.

Calvin reveled in *Lieutenant Emory Report's* scientific ambiance. His achievement led to his being asked to contribute a description of New Mexico plant life for the state Bureau of Mines and Mineral Resources publication *Mosaic of New Mexico's Scenery, Rocks, and History* in 1964. His last major publication was *Barnabas in Pittsburgh*, 1966. It is the story of the founder of a home for sick boys and men, a man who was the uncle of Calvin's second wife. It was self-published and is of limited interest except to a very few associated with the subject matter. Across his career he also contributed more than a hundred newspaper and magazine articles on religious, scientific, and cultural matters. Many of them deserve reprint.

There have been two commentators on Calvin of note. Lawrence Clark Powell wrote often and admiringly, L. G. Moses only once, but in a beautifully wrought essay introducing Calvin and his work and life to a select audience in a small regional church publication. Powell, however, had a wide audience through his many books on Southwestern literature, so his favorable mention of Calvin's work meant much. I am grateful to join their esteemed company.

It is pure serendipity that I would pause in my own spiritual quest at the Church of the Good Shepherd. I had left my *Roman* Catholic faith (Episcopalians are quick to point out that they too are Catholic) but thirsted for something that resembled it. This I find at Good Shepherd. It dawns on me that Ross Calvin did something similar in Pittsburgh. And now, deeply immersed as I have been in tracing out his life, I sometimes feel that I sense him at the altar where he spent fifteen years. Could his spirit be lingering still?

1

Learning Beckons

Ross R. Calvin at age four with parents Charles Fletcher Calvin, 35, and Addie Virginia Calvin, 29, in a photo taken in 1894. (Ross Calvin Papers, Center for Southwest Research, University Libraries, University of New Mexico)

Ross Calvin found his fame in the mountains and deserts of the American Southwest, but he came from solid Midwestern farm stock and bore a long and distinguished family name. The 1900 U.S. Census noted that his father, Charles F. Calvin, was the renter of 177 acres in Edgar County, Illinois, just nine miles west of the Indiana state line. He was forty-one at the time. His wife, Addie, was thirty-four. Ross R. Calvin was ten. Ross Randall Calvin had arrived November 22, 1889, some twenty-three months after the January 7, 1888, marriage of his parents, Charles Fletcher Calvin and Addie Virginia Propst. He was their only child. The census lists the father's profession as "farmer." His forebears followed a completely different line of work. The Calvins descended from French Huguenot boatmen in France. Ross Calvin noted that a religious refugee from Europe with the "incredible double-barreled surname of Luther Calvin" settled on the banks of the Delaware River around 1700 as a ferryboat operator. Always proud of his family name, he would have preferred his lineage trace back to the famed theologian John Calvin himself, but that was wishful thinking. From that foothold in the New World the Calvins spread west.

Ross did not come from a highly educated family. His mother, after country schooling, had been sent to Professor Purdy's Academy in Paris, Illinois, where, among other subjects, she studied Latin. Later Ross did the same, but with much more concentration. Calvin's father, by contrast, had other interests. There is no record of formal schooling. Apparently, his fondness for hard drink exceeded that for books. "His young manhood was not dissolute," wrote Calvin in a brief sketch of his father, "but he had a liking for liquor." One day, however, as Charles was out riding horseback with a party of other young men, he pulled the flask of whiskey from his pocket and hurled it into the bushes by the side of the road, vowing, "I'm through with it. I'll never take another drink." He never did.

The census listing young Ross Calvin took no note of any of this, of course. He was referenced only as "at school." That could be said of him for many years to come. The census also did not show that the boy was academically gifted and soon to be advanced two grades in what is known as a "double promotion" recognizing superior ability and intellect. It was a harbinger of his future scholastic promise. Nor did the census record how important nature was already becoming to the youth.

The family farm with its woodlots, creeks, and sloughs, with prairie land all around, was to become a living laboratory for him. L. G. Moses tells us that Ross's earliest recollection of the natural world occurred at age four, when he spied the tracks of a rabbit in the snow outside his bedroom window. The presence of a wild thing, which in the predawn hours had been so close, moved him in such a way that many years later he recalled in a letter to his grandchildren how his interest in nature was born on that chilly winter morning: "Never shall I forget the thrill it gave me."

Ross Calvin with classmates in his 1906 Chrisman High School photograph. He is in the first row second from right. (Ross Calvin Papers, Center for Southwest Research, University Libraries, University of New Mexico)

By age twelve he had begun recording his observations in Log Books, his name for the journals he kept the rest of his life. As he wrote his grandchildren many years later, "I began to jot down lists of such matters." He recalled for them a magical moment one hot June morning when he was about their age. He recounted the thrill of hearing "a dry rasping sound." That intrusion on his thoughts caused him to look down to the dead leaves at his feet. There he saw "a green snake. It was green!" Ross wrote that he had encountered many snakes since that time but never a green one. "In this way," he related, "any rare sight or sound might sometimes get itself permanently imprinted upon my attention."

Botany particularly attracted him. His only systematic study of the subject, he later recalled, was at Chrisman High School in the spring of 1905 and ended the same year. But he attained "a little more than average proficiency." He went on, "My long walks were even then in a real sense, botanical field trips, as they have been ever since." He was always learning and always thinking about what he had learned. Such study was to set him upon his life's path. For Calvin's observations of nature and his bent for learning led to a career in scholarship and writing, even though he ultimately chose a religious vocation over one in science.

Ross Calvin poses for his official high school graduation picture in a studio in Paris, Illinois. (Ross Calvin Papers, Center for Southwest Research, University Libraries, University of New Mexico)

Farm chores—slopping the hogs, splitting and fetching in firewood, and drawing water from the well—and leisure time activities—tramping the woods, hunting, and fishing—aside, Ross was a superior student and an outstanding track athlete. He graduated from high school in June 1906 as a member of a class of ten. Because of his earlier advancement, he was just sixteen and a half. The week of festivities included a party at which the graduates were treated to ice cream, cake, and candy. The culmination was a commencement address at the Chrisman Baptist Church (his grandmother's church) by Professor J. D. Shoop of the Holden School in Chicago on "The Strenuous Life." It was an apt description of what was to become the lodestone, the north star of Calvin's life. The other nine members of his class married and began working. He soon distanced himself from them.

This 1910 DePauw University yearbook picture of Ross Calvin was accompanied by the note, "Fond of the long green." Was Calvin overly fond of money as an undergraduate? (DePauw *Mirage* 1910)

His relative immaturity prompted his parents to keep him at home for a year and a half after high school until his physical and emotional growth could catch up with his intellectual level. Ross enrolled in the well-regarded DePauw University in Greencastle, Indiana, in January 1908, as a member of the class of 1911. Slightly more than half the students were women. Eighty-eight per cent were Hoosiers. Calvin attended during a rapid growth period in enrollment. Most occurred in his college (liberal arts), where enrollment soared from an average of 460 between 1900 and 1910 to nearly 800 in the decade following. While there is no record, Ross may have qualified for both athletic and academic scholarships. He ran on the school's 1909 and 1910 track teams, and, of course, his scholastic record was stellar.

Ross Calvin was a member of DePauw University's 1908–09 and 1909–10 track teams and is shown here with team members bottom row third from left. (DePauw *Mirage* 1911)

The DePauw University campus as Calvin knew it. (DePauw *Mirage* 1911)

The family helped as it could, meager as that help might be. Calvin's father in 1899 had moved into town to enter the drayage business, but shortly afterwards assumed a Standard Oil products distributorship. Both represented an increase in income over what he had earned farming. Still, it is unlikely he could have afforded his son's full tuition. The family's finances had improved, but they were now struggling with payments on a new house along with what they could contribute to Ross's college expenses. His mother was helping out with income derived from dressmaking. "It was a time of hard work and great sacrifice," Calvin wrote later of those days, "but my parents had confidence in the future and in me. In all the long years since," he continued, "I have never once lost the sense of obligation that their sacrifice in those days laid upon [me]."

When Ross boarded the train for college he carried two books with him in addition to the Bible. They were a volume of the complete works of Virgil and Thomas Carlyle's *Sartor Resartus*. The college yearbook *Mirage* shows him as a handsome young man with a pleasant smile and a full head of hair. (The smile he retained all his life; the hair was mostly gone by the time of his first pastorate.)

Ross Calvin (second from left) is shown in academic regalia for his 1911 class picture with a resume of his undergraduate activities accompanied by the quotation, "I can fight and swear, too." Was he a vulgar battler? (DePauw *Mirage* 1911)

Founded in 1837, the university was governed by the Methodist Book of Discipline, which forbade "use of alcoholic beverages, dancing, attending theatrical performances of any kind, or playing cards or billiards." Smoking naturally was taboo. Ross became active in the university's social fabric. An early effort at non-academic writing was composing the lyrics for a new university song. He also wrote an essay for the 1911 yearbook entitled "A Sketch of Friendship." Trying to find his path among colleagues in a milieu of more-or-less intellectual equals, he joined the Philo Literary Society, an important part of the university's political life. It was the club to belong to.

One of his fellow club members was Olive Adine Chilton. In this Brookston, Indiana, native Calvin met his intellectual equal and emotional center. Their ages were nearly the same. She was a half-dozen months younger—born April 2, 1890. Adine (she preferred to use just her second name) was secretary of the Philo Literary Society, the sophomore class, and Sodalitas Latina, a relatively young organization (1896) founded to make Latin students more familiar with the customs and habits of Roman society. He was a member of Tusitala, an organization of students "who like to write things." They proved a natural fit. Ross, who had heretofore recorded observations chiefly of nature in his Log Book, diverged from that practice on May 2, 1908, the day of DePauw's annual university picnic, with a single entry: "Adine!"

Ross Calvin was a member of Sodalitas Latina and is pictured in the club photo bottom row far left. Adine Chilton was also a member but does not appear in this photo. (DePauw *Mirage* 1911)

Ross Calvin belonged to Tusitala, a student organization at DePauw University of those "who like to write things." Given his future avocation, that was appropriate. He is shown bottom row far right. (DePauw *Mirage* 1911)

The couple's formal relationship began on a frosty winter's night in early February 1909 when they spent their first evening together following a campus function. "From that night onward, it is safe to say, he was never out of her mind, nor she out of his," he was to write later. "They were lovers" before long, though not in the sense the word is used today. Both were products of small town America, and one assumes theirs was a chaste relationship. Even a kiss would have been overstepping the bounds of propriety. "There begins the story of her devotion, which is perhaps unsurpassed in the world's literature," Calvin wrote. He could have said the same for himself.

Adine may have had feelings for him even earlier if the rather cryptic wording appearing beside her junior yearbook picture is any indication. It read: "A Presbyterian and follower of Calvin." The year before, the entry had read: "Of two men she's not afraid." Adine's later love letters, often in French or German, contained numerous amorous expressions. Their relationship, however, remained pure. It was not until a summer apart followed by a fall of proper courtship that she allowed him to call her Adine. They shared their first kiss at the end of the 1909 term. They did not decide to marry until the spring of their senior year. Their relationship was then on and off for several years. The causes were both financial and Ross's wavering over his religious vocation. Their love, however, was never in doubt.

The DePauw University yearbook observation concerning Adine Chilton is even more opaque than Calvin's. To what could "Of two men she's not afraid" refer? Were there two men in her life? Ross Calvin was one but the other? (DePauw *Mirage* 1910)

Adine Chilton (the yearbook misspelled her first name the year before) is shown in her official DePauw University senior class picture far right with the caption "A Presbyterian and follower of Calvin." It was a clever play on words. (DePauw *Mirage* 1911)

Adine graduated Phi Beta Kappa in June 14, 1911. Calvin did not receive his A. B. degree until completion of summer classes since he had entered the university later than she. Her degrees were in German and Latin; his in English literature and Latin. Already, he was preparing for further study. In order to gain money to pursue a graduate degree he took a teaching position in the

English department at Westfield (Indiana) High School for $90 a month. When he left for graduate school at Harvard in 1912 ("an opportunity he could not well let pass"), the *Chrisman Weekly Courier* remarked that "there are very few young men of Mr. Calvin's age [he was then twenty-two] who have come to the front [like he has.]"

At Harvard the young Calvin clearly felt at home. He was a young master's candidate in English during one of the more exciting periods in the venerable institution's history. He reveled in its rigorous scholarly environment under the watch of newly inaugurated president Abbott Lawrence Powell. George Lyman Kittredge and Bliss Perry were departmental stars, and fellow luminary George Santayana had just retired.

In the spring of 1913 Calvin shared his feelings with the folks back home in a front-page article headlined "Letter from the East" in the *Chrisman Weekly Courier*. Harvard's publicity department could scarcely have done better. He praised the "Harvard tradition, the sense of long-accustomed uses, and the feeling of great age and dignity." Calvin, the former track star, also pointed with pride to the institution's athletic program, lamenting only that seats at big football games with Ivy League rivals Yale and Princeton had "an unpleasant way" of costing $20 apiece. Calvin compensated for non-attendance at those venues by spending nearly every Sunday afternoon at Boston's galleries and museums, a luxury he did not have in Illinois or Indiana. Nonetheless, aside from tuition, which was $150, he thought other expenses to be no higher at Harvard than in western schools.

While he reveled in Harvard the university, he had little regard for classmates who regarded it as their private playground or as just another opportunity to socialize. "If a man has a great burden of money to trouble him," Calvin wryly observed, "Harvard is a capital place for him to find relief." The Gold Coast, one of Boston's elite areas, "will welcome him with open arms and fancy automobiles." The playboys, he wrote in an acerbic vein, are known by "their huge fur overcoats and receding foreheads and the way in which they do not carry off scholastic honors."

Calvin was not alone in such views. T. S. Eliot, John Dos Passos, and E. E. Cummings were there at the same time. Dos Passos's biographer Virginia Spencer Carr has written, "Most Harvard graduates considered themselves well educated and expected their sons to follow them to Cambridge, live in the same dormitories (the private dormitories on Mount Auburn Street's 'Gold Coast' maintained waiting lists so that sons might occupy the identical rooms their fathers had), and pursue like careers." One of T. S. Eliot's biographers, Lyndall Gordon, recorded of these elite, "'Triflers' abounded, young men who were satisfied with the 'gentleman's C' and took four-day weekends in New York," while a Cummings biographer remarked how he "and his friends loved to explore the bars and brothels of Boston. He took advantage of his newfound freedom, as he later recalled, to 'roam that surrounding world *sans peur*, if not *sans reproche*.'" Carr went on about this crowd: "The din that arose sporadically outside the Harvard gates provoked only mild discussion or controversy within the sanctum"—avant-garde art, as exemplified by the 1913 Armory Show's arrival in Boston, being a striking exception. Yet all three writers concurred with Calvin that for the true student Harvard was intellectually stimulating.

Unlike his years at DePauw, apparently Calvin made no effort to join the Harvard literati. During all his years of his regular academic studies, Calvin had been growing increasingly more interested in religion and in a religious vocation. He once even considered joining a monastic Roman Catholic order. This we learn from L. G. Moses. When he finally put all thoughts of Catholicism behind him, Adine exclaimed, "For this day I thank God." Now she could see a clear path to marriage.

Calvin in his Harvard robes with the notation: "Terrible! The young PhD from Harvard." (Ross Calvin Papers, Center for Southwest Research, University Libraries, University of New Mexico)

Upon receiving his master's in English, he took a year off to teach at Syracuse University. The experience was hard on his eyes: he read "nine feet and three inches of freshman themes." In 1914 he entered Harvard's doctoral program in English philology, receiving his PhD at the age of twenty-six. At last he held a scholarship. His unpublished dissertation was entitled *The Life and Works of John Oldham*. Oldham was an obscure seventeenth-century English satirical poet and translator previously unexplored, a perfect choice for an aspiring doctoral candidate looking for suitable dissertation material. Many years later, he was to describe the field of philology as "possibly the most interesting and pretty certainly the most useless science known to man." Yet, as he told an interviewer, obtaining it was rigorous and required a great deal of proficiency in classical and medieval literature and languages—Latin, Greek, Old French, Anglo-Saxon, Middle English, and Gothic—as well as modern German, Italian, and Spanish.

2

A Love Lost, A New Family Begun

Following graduation from DePauw, Adine spent three years teaching in the high schools of Albion and Wolcott, Indiana. In 1914, with World War I thwarting her plans for further study in Germany, she entered graduate school at Radcliffe. That put her nearer Ross. After a year there, during which she achieved distinction and a master's degree, she returned to Indiana to spend two more years teaching at Muncie High School. There, "her skill and gentle nature made her beloved as few teachers are ever beloved." As always, Calvin was to write, "Love was at the core of her life." He could not have placed her on a higher pedestal.

Following completion of his PhD, Calvin accepted an associate professorship in the English Department at the Carnegie Technical Institute in Pittsburgh, 1916–1918. He even found time for some creative writing. He submitted a story to *Atlantic Monthly* loosely based on *Romeo and Juliet* (the manuscript was not accepted). In that city were to occur a series of life-changing events. Adine joined him. By then, Calvin had decided to enter the ministry and had to pick a compatible church in order to complete the process. His reasons for joining the Episcopal Church reflect his sense of class distinction, perhaps picked up at Harvard. Charles Calvin recalls his grandfather Calvin's explanation that he "had decided the best people in town [Pittsburgh] were Episcopalians and that was how he decided to become an Episcopalian."

Adine followed Calvin in making his newly adopted faith hers as well, but her reasons were simpler: she wanted to accommodate Calvin in every way she could. She was confirmed in the Episcopal Church by the Right Reverend Cortlandt Whitehead, the bishop of Pittsburgh. In becoming Episcopalian, she turned her back on the Presbyterian Church to which she had belonged since girlhood. The Rector Wyatt Brown performed the long-postponed marriage on June 12, 1917, in Pittsburgh's Church of the Ascension. They were both twenty-seven. The newlyweds honeymooned in New York City's Hotel Martinique in a $6.90 a night room.

The young couple wanted to start a family. When Adine learned she was pregnant, they returned to Indiana to be nearer her parents. Her only child, Ross Randall Jr., was born May 31, 1918, in Lafayette and christened in that city's St. John's Church. After a summer in Indiana, the young family returned to Pittsburgh so Calvin could begin his new work as a lay assistant in that city's Church of the Ascension.

This photo of Adine Calvin and Ross Calvin Jr., was taken in Chrisman, Illinois, in August 1918. It is the last known surviving photo of mother and child. She died five months later. The note is apparently Calvin's; he thought the photo of their son "a misrepresentation." (Ross Calvin Papers, Center for Southwest Research, University Libraries, University of New Mexico)

This position provided an entry point into his chosen vocation. The next step, as he put it, was "the resolve to enter the sacred ministry." That resolve was soon to be tested in the most severe manner. The Spanish influenza pandemic of 1918 was one of the deadliest in modern history, claiming upwards of fifty million lives. Some 675,000 of those deaths were in the United States alone. Many of the victims were young and otherwise healthy. One was Adine Calvin, only twenty-eight, the mother of a six-month-old son. She died one week before Christmas 1918, just nine days after having been stricken. Ross was inconsolable. His newly accepted faith in the Episcopal Church, supported by the Ascension clergy, afforded some relief, but only some. He threw himself into those things that would distract him from the pain.

One of those activities was writing, to which he now turned to channel his grief. Following Adine's death and funeral, Calvin allowed his feelings to surface in a four-by-six-inch soft cover, self-published booklet called *A Mystical Bride*, a reference to the church as the Bride of Christ. It featured a frontispiece photograph of Adine, showing a lovely and determined young woman peering into a future that she would never experience. The booklet was a summation of Adine's last days, her death and funeral, intercut with prayers, literary allusions, and Latin quotations (fitting since both had immersed themselves in the study of Latin at DePauw). In the book, Calvin provided an account of her final days that even now is difficult to read because of how much of his suffering and distress is expressed.

This portrait of Adine Calvin, likely the last, is from the frontispiece of *A Mystical Bride*.

It had begun innocently enough. Shortly after midnight, on Friday, December 9, Adine awakened her husband complaining of severe back pains and stiffening fingers. At mid-day, December 10, with no signs of improvement, Calvin wrapped her in a steamer rug, took her in his arms, and carried her and their infant son to a waiting ambulance. At the door of their apartment he paused before a reproduction of Leonardo da Vinci's portrait of the face of Christ to offer a short prayer. Upon admission to St. Margaret's Hospital, Adine was found to have an alarming temperature of 104.4. A few hours later she was diagnosed with pneumonia. Soon after, Ross Jr. received the sentence of influenza.

By Saturday there was no improvement, no change in mother or son. Calvin began hearing an ominous rattle in his wife's throat. Two days later she hemorrhaged, with blood pouring from her mouth. Soon after, her left lung started filling, her heart began to weaken, and the doctors no longer offered any hope. During the entire time, out of caution Adine could not see her son although he was hospitalized in the same institution. His condition continued to steadily improve. One of Calvin's final acts of devotion to his dying wife was to place his fingers on the child's lips for a last kiss to carry to his mother. Calvin left the hospital for a short time to seek solitude. From a walk in the hospital grounds he was urgently summoned to Adine's bedside. He rushed there in time to hear her gasp twice before falling silent. "The [attending] priest fell on his knees and commended her soul to God."

It is helpful for an understanding of the Calvin family dynamics to fully appreciate the deepness of Calvin's love for Adine. Had she lived, Calvin's life (as well as his relationship to his first-born) would have been vastly different. Calvin gave four reasons for writing *A Mystical Bride*. First, he explained, it was an attempt to occupy his mind until time could dull his grief. Second, his hope was that Ross Jr. in it "might find...some faint impress of his mother's presence." Third, it was to serve as an offering for everyone who suffered and mourned the death of a loved one. Finally, it was an attempt to keep Adine's memory alive. Calvin opened with a quotation from Tennyson's *In Memoriam*: "Yet in these ears, till hearing dies," and began his narrative with "The broken lily lies—the storm is overpast," from Shelley's *Manual of Consolation for the Bereaved*.

After a chronology of his wife's illness Calvin harkened to Psalm 130, "Out of the depths, have I cried unto thee, O Lord," but not before reminding his readers, "Let no man sorrow for her who is become the bride of Christ." Calvin then recounted the melancholy trip to her home in Indiana for her burial. It had begun with his arrival at the station in Pittsburgh, where the waiting undertaker handed him the "red baggage check...stamped with the word CORPSE." The train soon began passing by familiar scenes with Calvin occupying the same sleeping car the couple had used on their way to Pittsburgh just a short time before her death. On this final journey home, Calvin recalled in his account, he had no need to ask in the morning if she had slept well.

Calvin's account of the trip to Indiana and of familiar sights and memories as he and his wife's coffin drew closer to her home in Brookston is painful to read. Spying from his train window a copse of familiar trees, "I had a fleeting image of that June night when once she and I walked beneath those oaks...and talked of our earthly parting, while the moon rose over that still field behind us. We told each other then that it would be bearable—*for we had lived*." It began to rain as the train neared Brookston, and, finally: "We were at home...the last sad homecoming."

The weather changed as the pallbearers, who had known Adine as a girl, gently lifted the coffin from the train to the platform. "I followed close behind her alone," Calvin remembered, "for it was raining. That slow December rain...." Later at the cemetery, after crossing "the December landscape" over which "a melancholy wind was blowing," Calvin sensed: "There seemed to be a harvest of deaths [in the sodden ground] for one grave was waiting, [and] another was being dug." Only nine years had passed between their first kiss and their final good-bye.

Calvin concluded with a quotation from the *Aeneid*: "*Sunt lacrimae rerum et mentem mortalia tangunt*" (These are the tears of things, and mortality cuts to the heart). Calvin recalled a Valentine's Day gift to her: a translation of a love scene in Gabriele D'Annunzio's *Francesca di Rimini* wherein Paolo and Francesca exchange their first kiss and a scene from Dante's *Inferno*. He remembered laboring for days on the translations, polishing and revising his work to perfection, before finally presenting it.

The details of her passing were reported in Chrisman; Calvin wanted people to know. Adine's death merited a column-length obituary in the *Chrisman Weekly Courier* in its January 3, 1919, edition. Calvin most certainly wrote it. The article revealed some surprisingly intimate details. It described her as a "delicate lonely child" until her family moved to Brookston when she was eight and where she spent the next nine years. Adine would have been pleased at the newspaper's observation that she was "always conscientious and capable" in the classroom.

A Mystical Bride was dedicated to Adine in "deathless love." Those words seem prescient. Although Calvin was to have two more wives and two more children, it would appear that his love for Adine influenced any relationship he was to have with his future families. How could anyone ever to measure up to her?

The pamphlet and the obituary are the only surviving concrete evidence of Calvin's deep, intense love for her. Nothing else about their all too short marriage remains save a few photos and an index of her letters to him. Anything else that may have existed, in keeping with his strong proclivity for privacy about family affairs, either he destroyed at the time or his elder son did in accordance with directive years later to be "sure to destroy everything that should not be left behind.... The dead have a right to expect this of us." Grandson Charles Calvin believes this remark pertained to the papers of Calvin's mother, not his own, but it is probably "an accurate" assessment of his value of personal privacy. Calvin later did the same with letters and "other reminders" of his second wife's "final, lonely bitter years." Anything Ross Jr. might have retained in defiance of his father's wishes was reduced to ashes when his home in Los Alamos, New Mexico, was lost in a disastrous fire in 2000.

Ross Jr. was another pressing concern that Calvin must have thought he was addressing as best he could at the time under the circumstances. Once the child recovered, he was taken to be with his maternal grandparents in Brookston while his father remained in the East. Sadly, Calvin's initial affection grew into a distancing between the two that gradually morphed into estrangement and for Ross Jr. an unarticulated bewilderment at having no parents in his life.

A warm note was the best Calvin could muster in lieu of a visit for the child's first birthday.

> To my little Boy,
> Few things could make me happier than being with you on your first birthday, but it cannot be. In your brief year of life much has happened—but you have been mercifully spared. May God grant you grace and wisdom and beauty and strength, Darling, and keep you always!
> Your father

Things were not to get better for child or father. For the most part Calvin's early involvement consisted of handing off the tot to grandparents. He had little choice but to rely on them. At that time, it would have been almost unthinkable for him to try to raise an infant on his own. The term "single parent" had not been coined and certainly not "single father." Calvin had neither time nor place in his life for young Ross Jr. except for a few visits and letters. He lived mostly with his maternal grandparents in Brookston for the first five years of his life, an arrangement that became increasingly unsatisfactory to Calvin. He made a final visit to Adine's parents before his son was old enough to begin school. Deeming the environment there "not suitable" (an assessment the grandparents apparently did not take well), Calvin decided to move his youngster to his parents' home in Chrisman on a permanent basis. Ross Jr. lived with his paternal grandparents until his high school graduation in 1935. This arrangement resulted in "some unpleasantness," and there seems not to have been any further contact between the two sets of grandparents, Ross Jr.'s son reports. The boy did spend some summers and holidays with his mother's parents, but it was Grandmother Calvin who emerged as the important figure in the boy's life, probably more so than any other caregiver.

Having his in-laws and then his parents serve *in loco parentis* created tensions between son and father. Calvin's visits to look in on his child were "rare events and pretty fearsome." Calvin was always finding fault with how the youngster was "being raised, what he was learning, what kind of manners he was being taught." Ross Jr.'s son says his grandfather would "speak badly of [Ross Jr.], terrify him, and go away." Still, the boy continued to yearn for his father. One Christmas season the *Chrisman Weekly Courier* ran its annual "Letters to Santa" section on the front page. Among them was one from little Ross Jr. In it he listed the toys he wanted but ended by asking Santa "to please bring something for my Daddie." The whole matter remains to this day a continuing source of family pain. Another family member recognizes that it "is never far from our thoughts, and it is not a comfortable one."

Meanwhile, back in the East, the young widower gratefully returned to those pursuits that would keep him from dwelling on his loss: work and study. During the travails of the influenza epidemic in Pittsburgh, Calvin continued to serve as a lay assistant. While not courting death, he did not dodge it either, frequently attending the bedsides of those who had been stricken. A Church of the Ascension bulletin records his disdain at contracting the contagion: "If during the recrudescence of the epidemic, I can be of service to any family, I trust you will call me." He continued, "With the physician should go the priest; and where the priest goes—why not I who aspire to the priesthood?"

Ross Calvin (circa 1922) in a biretta, usually worn by Roman Catholic clergy or sometimes Anglian or Lutheran clergy. It is not commonly worn by Episcopal priests today. (Ross Calvin Papers, Center for Southwest Research, University Libraries, University of New Mexico)

With Adine's death though, Pittsburgh became too painful an environment. After private study at the Church of the Ascension, Calvin was ordained to the deaconate and sought a change of venue. In 1920 he entered the General Theological Seminary in Manhattan. Soon he landed a plum assignment as curate at St. Agnes's Chapel in New York City's distinguished Trinity Parish. When his studies were completed, Bishop Whitehead ordained him to the priesthood in St. Mary's Church in Pittsburgh on June 19, 1921. Whitehead immediately assigned him the Mission of the Transfiguration in nearby Clairton. There Calvin, after looking after his own flock, began ministering after hours to immigrants who had no church of their own. This sort of thing—taking on another group of the spiritual needy—was to become a practice with him. It was more work than was expected of him, but he thrived on it.

Among the immigrants were Eastern Orthodox Syrians living in "Hunkey-town." Of that experience, Calvin was to write later that "somehow, I never did feel exalted; but rather—just sort of grateful." Following his first missionary experience, he returned briefly to St. Agnes's Chapel before heading to Geneva in upstate New York and his first pastorate, now with a second wife. He remarried for love, but he was also under a stricture from his church that required wedlock as a condition of accepting the assignment. Distraught as he was at Adine's death, Calvin had remained a widower just seven years.

Ross Calvin was always proud of his athleticism. Here he bats in a church softball game in Geneva, New York, in his first pastorate. (Ross Calvin Papers, Center for Southwest Research, University Libraries, University of New Mexico)

Calvin met and courted Grace Van Deurs Hance in New York City, where she was studying. She was a stylish young woman quite different from Adine in looks, learning, and demeanor. She was some ten years her husband's junior. Like him, Grace had strong ties to the Episcopal Church. Her uncle had founded the St. Barnabas Home for sick men and boys in Pittsburgh. As with any aspiring cleric fresh out of seminary in 1921, Calvin wanted his own parish. He was eager to show he was up to the challenge and to put his training to work. Following their marriage in late January 1925, with hearts full of expectations, he and Grace moved to Geneva, a city of a few thousand on the northern end of Seneca Lake.

Calvin tried to assimilate his firstborn into his new home, but Grace apparently saw the boy as ill-mannered and "lacking in social graces and propriety." The seven-year-old was an outsider, an ill-at-ease youngster from the sticks. She was Eastern bred with the advantages of a comfortably well-off family. The boy clearly was not. Ross Jr. had, after all, been raised by aging grandparents in rural Illinois, themselves lacking in her social graces. Ross Jr. might well have been the "little savage" Grace thought he was. Ross Jr. perhaps sensed this and blamed his stepmother for the animus that forever plagued father and son. However, it is well to bear in mind that she was, after all, a new wife, a parson's wife at that, and pregnant to boot. Grace Calvin was a month shy of her twenty-sixth birthday when Ross Jr. entered her home. His new half-brother, Rodney Provoost Calvin, came along just six months later, in 1926.

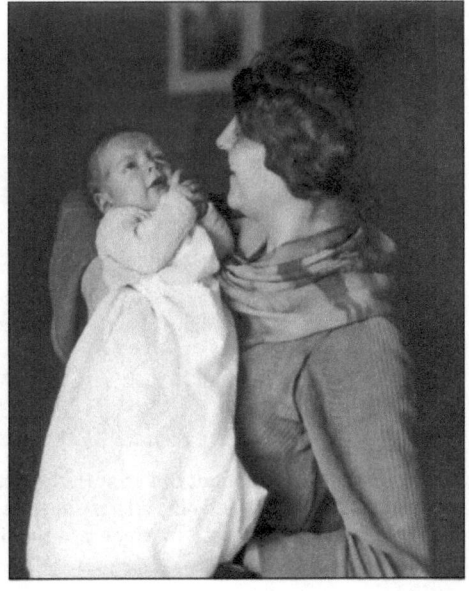

Young Rodney Provoost Calvin with his mother Grace for his first picture. (IHSF.org)

If Calvin's relationship with his firstborn was characterized by emotional abuse, that with Rodney seems to have verged, at least in the family's eyes, on physical abuse. Chastisement with a rubber hose is one example they remember. The adage about "sparing the rod and spoiling the child" was more the norm than the exception during Calvin's time, with harsh punishment, such as thrashings, not unexpected of good parents. Furthermore, as in the traditional family structure he had sprung from, Calvin was in his eye unmistakably the head of his family. He knew it and lost no opportunity to make sure the family knew it. His work—the church and his writing—came first. When the door to his study was closed, "the children knew to stay out."

An episode from this period illustrates Calvin's feelings toward Ross Jr. in his ongoing effort to make the boy strive to succeed as he had. "My father's recollection," says Charles, "was that Ross Jr. tumbled into a lake [perhaps at a church outing] and was floundering around in water deep enough to frighten him." Calvin saw his son in trouble but did not help; instead he kept pushing the boy back in (possibly in an ill-advised thought to help him overcome a fear of water or an attempt to make him swim): "A church member saw this, remonstrated with Calvin, and helped the boy out...." Charles believes that marked the end of any attempt to integrate the boy into Calvin's new family. Ross Jr. went back home to Illinois to be with his grandparents, never leaving them until high school graduation.

Ross Calvin Jr. bought this 1925 Harley Davidson model 74 for $40 in 1936. He was 18 years old. He recorded his purchase in an essay called "127 Teeth." Today the asking price for the classic machine is in the thousands of dollars. (Calvin Family)

Calvin did try to maintain contact with Ross Jr., the most estranged of an often-alienated group. And there were infrequent, but mostly unsatisfactory, attempts at trying to set the record straight. "You came to the home in Geneva in July 1925 at the age of seven. And you stayed behind in Chrisman with my father and mother when we came on west in early January 1927...and that, son, explains many, many things that happened afterwards. We never had a chance," he once wrote. All this was to set up a push-pull for Ross Jr. that was to forever torment him. "On the one hand," offers Charles, "he admired his father's intelligence, thought he was an important person, and wanted his approval. At the same time, there was a disappointment that he had not been included in his father's life and family, and there was this sense of rejection...." Grandson John Randall Calvin is of a similar mind. "There is "no question [Ross Jr.] felt abandoned," he says. He was "so wounded."

In his early thirties Ross Calvin wore the pince-nez in the popular eyewear fashion of the day. (Ross Calvin Papers, Center for Southwest Research, University Libraries, University of New Mexico)

Calvin had suffered from throat troubles for years. The long, harsh winters of his new home made them no better. A popular prescription of the day for such afflictions was sunshine; Calvin thought he knew where to find it. The Geneva newspaper told the story of his impending departure: "Rev. Ross Calvin to Leave the Ministry." The subhead read, "Rector of St. Peter's Church Tells Congregation That Failure of Voice

Makes It Impossible for Him to Continue Longer as a Priest." Calvin circled the words "as a Priest," and under it scribbled "No, No!" Yet the newspaper was reflecting Calvin's own words.

He had told a startled Sunday morning congregation that his voice had been failing for more than a year: "Sunday after Sunday I left the church almost without a voice when the service was over." Even though there had been "periods of partial relief," he simply did not feel up to another month of the "same aggressive effort." All this, the thirty-seven-year-old priest confided, left him "seriously handicapped in my parish activities." Calvin told his listeners he had hoped "to get through the ordeal without abandoning the sacred ministry." He said that hope had "now passed." Calvin told his congregation that when "I leave St. Peter's church, I shall cease to be what I have loved to be—a parish priest."

This remark is puzzling because Calvin knew he was not leaving the Episcopal Church, that he was not even going to leave its payroll for that matter since he had been licensed by Bishop F. B. Howden of Albuquerque on December 12, 1926, a few days before his public announcement in Geneva, to serve in the Missionary District of New Mexico and Southwest Texas (now the Episcopal Diocese of the Rio Grande).

If Calvin thought he was transferring to a sinecure in some sleepy outpost of the church as a missionary to some fifty communicants, he soon was to be relieved of that notion. As he was quickly to find out, the size of his congregation meant little in terms of the aggregate of duties he was expected to perform week in and week out. They varied little. He gave a sermon every Sunday whether ten heard it or twenty. He wrote and printed the church bulletin whether five read it or fifty. He liaised with the vestry. He performed funerals and weddings, although the latter were fewer in number during the Great Depression as more and more couples deferred wedded bliss until times got better. He met with the women's club, and so forth. The number of beneficiaries of his ministrations was smaller, but the duties were not. They could, and would, grind anyone down over time.

3

Leaving "The Known World": The Silver City Years

A dashing young couple Ross and Grace Calvin pause
for the camera in August of 1927. (IHSF.org)

Calvin's first view of his new hometown of Silver City, New Mexico, where he expected to stay just a few months but remained fifteen years, is enlightening: "We have left the known world behind," he confined to his journal, January 9, 1927, on the train west from a Christmas holiday visit to Chrisman. Young Ross Jr., just eight and a half, had been "dropped off" in

Chrisman with his Calvin grandparents as his father and stepmother made their way west with Rodney. The older boy described it as their "primitive home." Maybe by comparison with the rectory in Geneva it was; maybe it was the boy's feelings coming out at even more abandonment. The Geneva experiment had failed. After moving to Silver City, the elder Calvin had "no time for things of the past," especially his first son. There is no documentation Ross Jr. ever visited them in Silver City. Grandson Charles Calvin says he has "no idea how much was [Grace's] reluctance, [how much Calvin's] reluctance, or just inertia."

Grace Calvin poses for the camera in this photo taken soon after moving to Silver City. (Calvin Family)

Young Rodney Calvin at about age one and a half is admired by his adoring mother Grace Calvin, in this late autumn 1928 photo. (IHSF.org)

The town was alien to Calvin at first. He marveled at the scene the bustling station presented: lanky cowboys wearing wide-brimmed tall hats strolling alongside the once-a-day train from Deming, mingling easily with young dandies in straw boaters, drummers with their sample cases of wares, and women attired in their traveling best. The latest model roadster shared curb space with horses hitched nearby. He found an eclectic mix in the town of 3,500—health seekers, ranchers, college professors, and mining men. There were some whose professions were not advertised, such as the brothel keepers. Among the ethnicities were Anglos, Hispanics, and some Chinese. The Eastern-educated scholar and preacher made it sound in his writings as if he were approaching an abyss. Five years later he was to write, "Well do we remember that day when we stepped off the train.... Depressed and full of foreboding."

Ross Calvin had little leisure time from his duties as rector of the Church of the Good Shepherd in Silver City. When he did, he enjoyed donning casual attire and listening to news on the family radio. (IHSF.org)

Quickly he was installed as the new rector of the Church of the Good Shepherd. He had just turned thirty-seven. He had gone to Silver City as a "final experiment" seeking relief from a persistent sore throat—a potential career-ender for a preacher. As a son-in-law wondered many years later, "Is there anything more worthless than a preacher who can't talk?" The bracing mountain air and abundant sunshine of his new home soon cured him of his sore throat. Unfortunately, that affliction was replaced by insomnia, which plagued him for years. Stress resulting from overwork and family and money concerns surely contributed. Grandson John Randall Calvin says he "can only imagine the stress he put on himself to accomplish what he did." Given the debilitating nature of the affliction, one marvels at the impressive amount of work he was able to accomplish. Calvin simply did not let anything get in the way of working toward his goals.

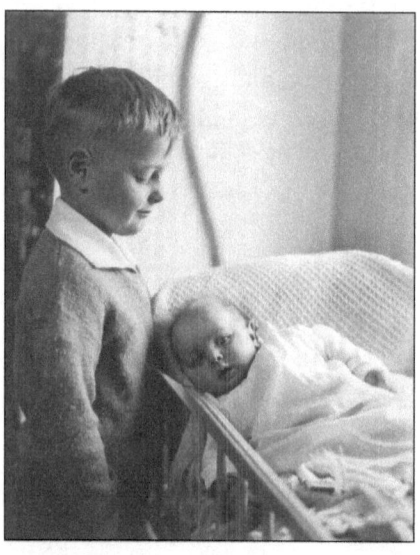

Big brother Rodney and baby sister Margaret (Peggy) in the family home in Silver City at Christmas 1930. She was about two and one half months old. (IHSF.org)

Margaret (Peggy) Calvin at play in the family yard in Silver City. This photo was taken on her second birthday. (IHSF.org)

Margaret Van Deurs Calvin, universally known as Peggy, joined the family in 1930, a beautiful blonde-haired Shirley Temple look-alike with a winning smile. She was Grace's second and last child. Her mother was then thirty-one. She and Calvin had what many couples yearn for: a boy and a girl. Her big brother doted on her, but as Rodney matured he successively took up the boyhood pursuits of his friends in Silver City: building model airplanes of bamboo and paper, kicking the football around in the front yard, and hunting in the nearby mountains.

Rodney Calvin enjoyed typical boyhood pursuits of his time. One was building model airplanes of bamboo and tissue paper. (IHSF.org)

Family helped pay for trips east for Grace Calvin and her children Rodney and Peggy who enjoyed their time at the seashore. (IHSF.org)

Little is known of Grace during this period, aside from routine duties in the home and her role as parish first lady, and for her occasional periods of illness that required hospitalization at least once. She colored some of her husband's photographs and took some of her own, she accompanied him on trips by foot and horse to the mountains, she kept house, and she entertained when Calvin's responsibilities called for it. She was deeply in love with her new husband as expressed in her letters. One began, "My beloved one," adding that "long have I loved these simple words so I give them to you." She urged her husband to accept them from her "heart's deepest chambers."

Grace Calvin and her children in their finery for a visit with her family. (IHSF.org)

Both Calvins were accomplished photographers. He used that skill to illustrate the first edition of *Sky Determines*. Their pictures were shown in a downtown gift shop. Her work was shown in an exhibition at Stanford University as well, and he showed his in the State Art Museum in Santa Fe. Ernie Pyle remarked on its quality, as did others who were to see it later in Calvin's books. Calvin complemented his interest by writing on photography. His musical interests, particularly the organ, were beginning to assert their side as well.

Popular visitors with the Calvins in Silver City were newspaper columnist Ernie Pyle and his wife Geraldine (Gerry) posing on November 9, 1939 with the coupe in which they toured the country searching out material for his columns. (IHSF.org)

Calvin had to find a "sense of release and freedom...from a troubled world," says Thomas O'Connor. Photography and music could provide that. So could the forests, mountains, and desert, to which he retreated as often as possible. Sometimes he would take his family along as he unwound. In a June 1932 column for the *Silver City Independent*, Calvin described an idyllic afternoon and evening along the banks of the Gila River with Rodney, then about six. "After supper I make a willow whistle for The Boy. He toots and toots. Then, as the young moon rests on the western cliff, he falls asleep, his head on my knee." Likely Grace and Peggy were there too although the article does not mention it.

Calvin charted his progression from pilgrim health seeker to accomplished self-trained amateur botanist. "We were supposed to spend much time out in the sunshine," he wrote. While they did so, "everywhere we noticed strange plants, the cacti [a favorite]." As a transplanted Easterner, all the plants he encountered were new to him. But he quickly immersed himself in learning to recognize them. Thus, when a Silver City housewife presented him with a flower she had found and packed in a handful of moist dirt, he was able to identify it at once as a lady's slipper. Then, as befitted his vocation, he went on to reflect how the little sphere of dirt represented "a kind of resume and symbol of the ball of earth on which we live and move and have our being."

Ross Calvin posed his beautiful young wife Grace out in the New Mexico sunshine for this artful photo among his favorite flora, the cacti. (IHSF.org)

His demanding profession required an occasional refuge. His work load was crushing. In an outline of his duties at Good Shepherd and his concomitant assignment at St. Luke's in Deming, he devoted a page headed "Misc. ministrations." It was packed. He cited keeping in "pastoral touch" with families scattered across a wide expanse of southwestern New Mexico— from the tiny mining town of Mogollon in the high mountains to the desert community of Lordsburg, a distance of some 115 miles, some of it tortuous driving—to ministering to prisoners (a duty he held dear), to making hospital calls, often to patients with no connection to Good Shepherd. He participated in community activities such as Scouting and Rotary; he developed as many contacts "as possible" at the local college; and he received callers "of all ranks, on all kinds of errands from everywhere." Finally, he maintained a heavy correspondence, read widely, studied, and meditated so as "to compress the results into 20 minutes for Sunday." Calvin's correspondence alone would have taxed anyone. Five years after coming to Silver City, Calvin assumed editorship of the *Southwestern Churchman* and contributed many articles to it over several years. He had a wry outlook on his new assignment: "If you can get people to read religious literature, you can get them to read anything."

Ross Calvin and Grace escaped to the Gila Country whenever his church duties would allow. Here they are below the summit of Whitewater Baldy at nearly 11,000 feet in the Mogollon Mountains in June of 1931. (IHSF.org)

As the years passed, Calvin's Silver City Log Books increasingly reveal a man at home in his new environment, a pastor tending his flock, a new transplant at ease among his somewhat rough-hewn newfound Western friends, and a student of nature increasingly more comfortable and excited by the challenge of his outdoor surroundings. They also depict a man highly productive and successful in his writing.

One group that did not receive Calvin's sympathy was the down-and-outers who lived in and around Silver City during the Great Depression. L. G. Moses has called him "an elitist by nature and intention." On April 22, 1933, in his "The Village Parson" column in the *Silver City Daily Press* Calvin wrote: "We have observed that the Forgotten Man, once he gets acclimated to relief, tends to degenerate into a mere shovel leaner." That was a label he hung more than once on those he thought should be looking after themselves instead of relying on government subsidies. Calvin did see President Roosevelt's New Deal programs as "necessary evils" to assist victims of the country's economic disaster. But he feared these "shovel leaners" were destroying America's self-reliance. Only traditional rugged individualism, he believed, would keep the country safe and strong.

At times Calvin seemed to lump welfare recipients with another type of the disenfranchised—the tramp. As he confided in a pair of "Village Parson" columns in 1938, one of the reasons he so heartily disliked these self-styled "Kings of the Road" was that "in a world of bitter experience, I have never found one with a word of gratitude for anybody...." Still, Calvin's grandson John Randall believes his grandfather made "an effort to reach out to those less fortunate" despite his rhetoric.

There was one notable exception to Calvin's general scorn. He exhibited great compassion for enrollees of the Civilian Conservation Corps camps. In a two-column article, entitled "Ministrations in the C.C.C. Camps," he explained why he admired the camps and their undertaking. Aside from providing much needed employment, Calvin said he thought it was "much more important" to discover the "permanent effect, if any," of the endeavor on the participants themselves. Curiously, he did not address the question of the program's impact on the environment. Six hundred young men, affectionately known as "woodpeckers," labored in three camps around Silver City, installing culverts, thinning the forest, and implementing erosion control, a task they called "gully plugging." All these were recognized forest management tools still being used today. They did all this for a dollar a day with rough-and-ready accommodation under canvas and wool blankets to keep out the mountain chill and plenty of fresh wholesome food to fill their stomachs.

While he conceded that some of the program's participants were coarse and did not belong to "a Congregation of the Spotless," Calvin observed that most were average—subject to the same situations and conditions they would be at home. Some became ill and were taken to the Fort Bayard hospital outside town, where Calvin visited them. Others got in trouble, were locked up, and Calvin went to see them in jail: "they are friendless and I try to be a friend," he explained. Calvin, in asking what a chaplain could do, provided an answer: "To one who knows forest and mountains and loves them well," he wrote, "an introductory step is obvious—to try to disseminate the same feeling in the Corps, and to see that here the contact of the earth, through pines and sun and soil, achieves its accustomed beneficial results."

On the whole, Calvin saw the CCC undertaking as a back-to-the-earth movement defining "a social experiment of first magnitude importance" by combining military discipline (the camps were overseen by Army Reserve officers) and civilian labor. Calvin took the opportunity to observe that all this was occurring against the backdrop of a nation that was "striving for a return" to the "stalwart muscularity of earlier decades." So far as we know, Calvin tried his hand at fiction only rarely, but, interesting enough, a never submitted novel, *Mr. Fairchild Sleeps*, a father-son relationship story dating from the mid-1930s, was set partly in a CCC camp.

In 1932 he addressed the Silver City Rotary Club, of which he was president on the topic "Thinking Toward the Future: A Thoughtful Consideration of What New Mexico Can Do With Her Resources of Climate, Scenic Beauty and Historic Interests." Climate was first on his list of attractions. He began by saying that it was time "thoughtful people" realized that "New Mexico is different." He then enumerated the reasons. Some were positive, others were not. One remedy for the state's economic plight he suggested was to "industriously develop" all possible mines and ranches, all possible manufacturing—"it won't be much." He offered another possibility: tourism, which today is one of the main drivers of the state's economy. "[B]y accepted standards," he wrote, the state was a poor place to make a living—"but what a gorgeous place to live!" His listeners were especially concerned about how they and their neighbors could extricate themselves from the grips of the Depression, which was wreaking economic, social, and personal havoc among them. In addressing that issue, he admitted the odds against them: "New Mexico lacks great cities...and lacks the resources that would create great cities in the future," he observed, and "by reason of its economic handicap, it will probably remain near its present position—in forty-fifth place among our national commonwealths." He granted that although New Mexico was "an unlikely theatre for fortune-makers, it has compensations." Some of Calvin's ideas were eventually adopted. He proposed a department of Southwestern Studies in the state's universities. Today, a master's degree in that field is offered at New Mexico Highlands University. He also suggested increased promotion of Native American and Hispanic arts and crafts; this too has been institutionalized as well, with annual celebrations in Santa Fe and other cities. He tried to end on a positive note, holding that New Mexico has much that makes life worthwhile.

Ross Calvin and daughter Margaret Van Deurs Calvin (Peggy). As she became old enough, she sometimes accompanied her father to the outdoors. (John Randall Calvin)

One of the earliest examples of Calvin taking on a paid writing assignment was for the United States Soil Conservation Service in 1935. He was named in the U.S. Department of Agriculture's Miscellaneous Publication No. 233, List of Technical Workers, as an assistant soil conservationist. His role was to provide a historical introduction to the government's report on the Upper Gila watershed. Calvin wrote that the story of man's "use and misuse" of the land was the "most neglected while at the same time one of the most important phases" of history. His aim was to provide "a comprehensive guide" for the watershed's rehabilitation in the here and now and "a philosophy" for its use in the future. He warned that users must understand that the watershed's "safety and stability" tomorrow rest "upon foundations laid today" and that the present store of "nature's gifts is not inexhaustible." Calvin based his report from an entirely new vantage point—the air. His Log Book provides flight details. A photo shows him in typical flight garb of the day—leather helmet, fur-lined leather jacket, and high boots—standing by a Ford trimotor ("Tin Goose") flown in from Los Angeles to provide the ten-minute flight over the San Vicente arroyo and its tributaries.

Ross Calvin in one of his favorite places: the outdoors. (IHSF.org)

Calvin was playing the stock market from the 1930s onward and, like most investors, he was lamenting his losses. He noted that "the price of my stocks [is] dropping steadily day after day." There is no record of where he found the money either to dabble in the market or later to underwrite his share of publishing his first book. It is possible Calvin used fees (meager as they were) from publishing various articles to bankroll his investments on Wall Street. Grace's family might have given her some money as well. He continued this practice well into retirement and was a meticulous record keeper of both church and personal expenditures. In financial straits throughout the Depression, he even mentions in his diary that he substituted for the church janitor when she was unable to perform her Saturday duties and pocketed the dollar or so she would have earned from dusting the pews, sweeping the floors, and putting copies of the Book of Common Prayer back in their proper place. His penchant for detailed record keeping presents an anomaly concerning the amount of revenue he earned from the 1934 edition of *Sky Determines*. The first printing was sold out. He shared half the proceeds, yet he does not record, with one exception, how the royalties were spent.

4

Sky Determines

Ross Calvin wrote a handful of books and hundreds of articles during his long literary career but nothing as important as his first book, *Sky Determines: An Interpretation of the Southwest.* Its publication in April 1934 brought him widespread recognition as an interpreter of New Mexico and the Southwest. The book changed his life in a positive way save for the gratuitous stress that accompanies achievement. Calvin at the time was just a few months shy of his forty-fifth birthday. Usually the words *fame* and *fortune* are coupled to indicate a certain measure of success. In this case the fortune part of the equation, as noted, has to remain unanswered because there is no record from Calvin or Macmillan, his publisher, showing sales and royalties. He made a personal notation of one payment and that was all. On January 1, 1936, Calvin cashed a royalty check to buy a Zeiss magnifier for his plant studies.

For a book such as this, publication was a risky venture in those bleak Depression days. It was a gamble not to be undertaken lightly. As a result, Macmillan's editorial board mulled over the project at length but finally concluded that the manuscript was "an unusual and interesting" piece of work that "deserved publication." In September 1933, Lois Dwight Cole of Macmillan wrote Calvin's agent, J. N. Masterton, that the publisher wished "circumstances were such that we were not forced" to suggest a cost-sharing arrangement. Her colleagues, she explained, thought the book "so distinctly" of a type that the company wanted it on its list—but with a condition. She hoped Masterson understood the difficulties of publishing "eminently worthwhile but not popular" books in "these times." All this was a lead-up to the publisher's proposal: Macmillan felt that the poor economic conditions of the day forced it to ask Calvin to bear half the publication costs so that the firm and Calvin, perhaps with an "interested association," would share the risks. Calvin complied, although it is unclear where he got the money. It is highly plausible that Grace's family helped.

The original cover of the 1934 edition of *Sky Determines*. (The Macmillan Company)

One wonders what Calvin thought of the book when it finally emerged from the printer. It is rather nondescript in appearance with a light tan cover 8½ x 5½ (20.32 x 13.97 cm), consisting of 354 pages and ten black and white photographs, all but one taken by Calvin and Grace. The cover, back cover, and spine feature alternating Pueblenos sun and summer rain symbols in red. It sold for $3.50, a dollar more than a high-quality men's shirt. (Unsigned first editions now go for $50; signed editions much higher.) *Sky Determines* launched him as a first-rate Southwestern writer.

The gamble the publisher and author shared paid off—at least from a literary point of view. The book was met with dozens of positive, even effusive, reviews from coast to coast as well as abroad. The second word of the title received much attention. Calvin had wanted to be recognized for his objective approach. Exploring determinism provided that opportunity. *The Times Literary Supplement*, in noting the book's "curious title," observed that Calvin had employed the verb "in the fullest sense of the word" to underscore that it meant everything in New Mexico's life. The newspaper also praised Calvin for writing "learnedly and lucidly."

Lawrence Clark Powell was to later call it "an unrelenting theme" as Calvin followed the sky's all-determining influence on ecology, anthropology, history, and economics through the rolling millennia of New Mexico. Calvin later paraphrased himself, saying New Mexico's "cultures come from its heavenly climate." Determinism is also an unfolding of out-and-out cause and effect: i.e., every phenomenon has a cause, and this relationship is predictable given enough information. For Calvin, the priest, scientific determinism eliminated supernatural causes beyond the scope of his religious convictions; determinism meant biological, behavioral, cultural, and environmental, or climatic determinism, folded into one with a stress on the latter. Powell was so enamored of the verb "determines" and its appropriateness that he used it himself at three key points in *Southwestern Book Trails: A Reader's Guide to the Heartland of New Mexico & Arizona* (1982). He does so when speaking of the importance of Southwestern rivers, observing that rivers *determine*; the same of mountains, to note that they *determine*; and finally to conclude that books describing the region do indeed *determine*.

L. G. Moses makes several important observations concerning Calvin's reliance on determinism. According to him, one work noted for its environmental determinism that Calvin used extensively was Walter Prescott Webb's *The Great Plains* (1931). Echoing others, Moses wrote that Calvin's thesis "was really nothing new." What *was* new, he said, was that *Sky Determines* was "the author's celebration of his new homeland." Calvin's gift to the literature of the Southwest, Powell argues, was "his ability to convey his scientific knowledge to the general reader in a manner that was both pleasing and articulate."

Calvin's view of determinism, in Silver City writer Tom Hester's view, is not as "mechanical" as Walter Prescott Webb's approach because Calvin's "thinking had a more multivarious cast." He expands, "Most of us today take for granted things like interactions as a normal way of understanding our world." Hester though asserts that Calvin was "there ahead of us," like "his hero" Lieutenant W. H. Emory, "observing and explaining what he saw, preserving the complexity in simplicity." Hester does note Calvin's lack of "the particular" that Mary Austin frequently exhibited in *The Land of Little Rain*, but then she did not have his view of determinism.

In the opening section, "Theme Stated," Calvin explains, "Climate effects an intelligible unity." In New Mexico, he tells us, "History has not taken place under a roof," hence "the sky, as [the] source of life-giving moisture and of the desert-making heat, determines not only its plant and animal life, but has created the peculiar environment, which until the introduction of driven wells...determined likewise the direction of its human activities and pursuits." After stating his overarching idea, Calvin devotes four chapters to the New Mexico and Southwestern natural world (the sky and its interface with desert, mountains, and forest), then six to those impacted by them (the "Forgotten Peoples," the Conquistadores, Pueblños, Mexicanos, Apaches, and ranch men), and finally a chapter on human devices that made life bearable and productive—wells and trails, such as the El Camino, the Santa Fe, and the Butterfield, and their modern counterparts, the highways, railroads, and airways. The book is a well conceived, well wrought tale, perhaps the more compelling when considered from the standpoint of its importance today.

In discussing the workings of nature, his writing can attain poetic flair. In describing the advent of the monsoons west of Silver City one afternoon on June 12, 1933, and the heralding of its attendant thunder, he writes: "Presently a sound fell from the sky as though someone were moving heavy furniture in the attic." He shows us how a mountain stream works like a fish working its way upstream: "It eddies and stands on end, it foams and leaps with various antics...." Then, switching metaphors, he depicts the water's action as grinding downstream bottoms to bedrock, leaving the granite "polished like a clean table."

Calvin shows how weather works, then demonstrates its impact as a type of domino effect on those who live under its influence. Despite his emphasis on sky, Calvin was much taken with how mountains play their role. He calls them "weather breeders." Meteorologists understand what he was driving at. U.S. Weather Service forecaster David Hefner of the Santa Teresa, New Mexico, station underscores that mountains "modify" existing weather patterns. Fellow meteorologist David J. Novlan, the climate focal-point specialist with the National Weather Service Forecast Office in El Paso, concurs, adding that Calvin's ideas about mountains are "for the most part correct." New Mexico, he explains, is home to the southernmost chain of the Rocky Mountains. They keep the very bitter cold Arctic air to the east. In addition, the mountains provide lift. Any moisture with a storm system "wrings out" precipitation on the windward side. Eighty years earlier, a non-meteorologist priest and philologist had the same view and had used almost exactly the same words. Calvin observes that when the saturation point in a storm is reached, some of the moisture is "squeezed out." Mountains have their role; they determine, Calvin believed, but only in a limited way.

His observations about the summer rainy seasons, which New Mexicans today call "monsoons," are as true today as when he penned them. He calls the long-awaited summer rains "second springtimes." Meteorologist Novlan affirms what Southwesterners already know: "The North American Monsoon is extremely important" because it brings at least fifty percent of the region's annual precipitation. The problem, as he casts it, is that the precipitation is "rarely evenly distributed" and comes in the form of thunderstorms, which often result in localized flash flooding. This phenomenon can be terrifying and sometimes deadly. Unsuspecting motorists or hikers sometimes lose their lives.

New Mexico, especially the southern region, has three monsoon seasons although they may not be as apparent as the moisture-laden version. The dry monsoon in March and April comes with southwest winds, strong gusts, and blowing dust. The one New Mexicans recognize during July into September brings moisture from the Gulf of Mexico. This is what "most people think about when they think Monsoon," says Novlan; it is analogous to the Indian monsoon. Finally, the cool monsoon from October to February brings the prevailing winds that are more west to north. These can bring snow.

Calvin was no desert dweller, but he respected and recognized the critical role it also plays in shaping New Mexico weather. "Nowhere," he writes, "is the sky's determination so emphatically sharp as on the desert." His home in Silver City was fewer than fifteen miles from Hurley to the southeast with a drop in elevation of some four hundred feet, yet a world apart. There the countryside rapidly begins to take on the look of the desert—expanded vistas, tumbleweeds replacing trees, and springtime (monsoon) winds blowing dust that sometimes darkens the landscape like nighttime, forcing drivers to take special care lest they lose their way and stray into the path of an oncoming vehicle with sometimes deadly results.

But New Mexico and the Southwest are not all desert, contrary to what many think. Calvin was sensitive to the Easterner's "vulgar error" in believing the American Southwest was "everywhere and over all desert." Nonetheless, he knew it as "a place where no life form survives without special adaptation to aridity." In the desert, he was aware, excess heat and extreme evaporation combine with a scarcity of rainfall to "produce a complete though one-sided responsiveness." He warns that "a man at grips with the desert...finds it a red-eyed savage."

Like John C. Van Dyke, whose work inspired him in so many ways, Calvin was stirred to wield some of his keenest observational and descriptive skills on the interplay of the desert's plant life with the ever-present wind. He provides us with another simile so that we see the "fugitive tumbleweeds begin to race like fleeing animals." But the story is not confined to the desert. If it were to deprive us of moisture, he reasoned, there has to be a counterbalance. That caused him to see that the mountains and forests work together to conserve and dispense moisture. A wise beholder, he observes, "must be impressed" with the mountains' role in storing snowfall for the watershed's drier months. "Then the forest serves as its conservator." He presents us with a broad picture played out on a grand scale in a fascinating and challenging landscape.

Calvin realized, however, that in order to tell a complete story of his new homeland he had to begin at the beginning. He thus begins with the "Forgotten Peoples"—the aborigines, those who came first by whatever name they were to be called. Ever mindful of his thesis, Calvin shows that climatic conditions (insufficient rain) "anchored" these first peoples to areas where water could be found. From this permanence grew "many notable consequences"—literally everything. The "Forgotten Peoples" over time were able to develop systems of governance, agriculture, art, architecture, clothing, and religion. "This progress in comfortable and secure living," Calvin notes, "began in prehistoric times and continues to the present. It is the direct result of climatic environment." If there is little or no rain, find another way: drill or use drip irrigation.

After the "Forgotten Peoples" came others. They cared for little but gold. They were driven by stories of wealth conveyed to them by others. These were the conquistadores, who were the first Europeans to encounter the "Forgotten Peoples." After traveling hundreds of weary, thirsty miles to the Rio Grande it was easy, says Calvin, for the Spaniards to understand the "reasonableness" of the Puebleños' worship of the "Sky Powers" (the sun and water). After all, the sky had determined their routes of exploration along water trails (rivers), passing at times near the silver and gold they fervently sought without knowing it was there.

Calvin posits this corollary: "Suppose…Oñate…had come marching up the Gila instead of the Rio Grande, and founded his settlement not at Santa Fe but at Silver City." One can ponder the consequences. The answer to his speculations can be summed up in one word—aridity. Calvin writes that the sky determines that New Mexico has no navigable waterways because of inadequate rainfall. Without metallic treasure, New Mexico was not worth the trouble to the Spanish crown. As for the heathen souls residing there, only the Church cared.

From discussion of the "Forgotten Peoples" and the conquistadores, Calvin transitions to the Puebleños. He adds little further to our understanding except for postulating on the role the "Sky Powers" played for both the invaded and the invader. The sky again determined everything, he insists. The Spanish padres were forever attempting to abolish the rain gods, and the Puebleños were forever striving to retain them. As Calvin speculates, "There is reason for believing that by means of a great climatic pulsation [El Niño and La Niña in today's terminology] the 'Sky Powers' themselves took a definite part in fomenting trouble for the Spaniards."

As much as the Spaniards were severely disadvantaged by weather and as much as Calvin admired them, he cared little for their descendants. His chapter on "Mexicanos" reflects a certain racism. "Mexican" was a derogatory, inaccurate slur, even if it did reflect contemporary usage and thought. His subject matter was not Mexicans (e.g., citizens of Mexico), but those known today as Hispanics or Latinos. Blaming New Mexico's lack of productivity on the climate is one thing; blaming it on the inhabitants is another. New Mexico's story, Calvin says, was fated to be that of an arid, barren land because of scarcity of rain. "The land's aridity was not merely an inert obstruction. It gave active opposition." It is difficult to argue with these observations. But then he strays into dangerous, biased ground when he observes that the conquistadores, for lack of suitable racially pure partners, "mated where fancy led them" with "Indian squaws," leading to a race of "half breeds." It was, for him, a "grading down of the human stock." Remarking that it is "futile to contend" that most of the Mexican population is of the same strain as those who marched with Coronado, he likens them to "poor whites." He goes on, "placidly they drift," exhibiting "unprogressive indolence."

To support his beliefs Calvin quotes a University of Oklahoma professor that "Mexicans" were below normal weight and height because they "eat too many beans." He attempted, he says, to "comprehend with compassion" their hard life in Depression times from poor nutrition, hard work, and few creature comforts. But Calvin persisted in his belief that "Mexicans" were inferior and said so in many ways in *Sky Determines* and elsewhere. It was to be many years before he received his comeuppance, but receive it he did— fittingly enough at the hands of Mexican-American scholar J. Ortega, editor of *The New Mexico Quarterly Review*. Calvin recanted and attempted to explain and apologize for his misconceptions. He did seem to understand that "where the bounty of nature is scant [i.e., little rainfall], human effort does not much avail" regardless of the steward's race.

Calvin's ethnic favorite was the Indian, who, he erroneously wrote, "in spite of much propaganda to the contrary is not badly treated" by Washington. Calvin exalts particularly in the fierce, racially pure Apache, the "falcons of the desert." He calls them "a great people." For him, the Apaches are "nature's supreme adaptation to [an] arid environment." He admires their incredible feats of survival and holds that their struggle with those of European stock was "a running sore." They were "not so much defeated as overwhelmed" by their adversaries' strength of numbers and access to water. "In the end," he writes, "water and the lack of it played the trump cards." Calvin does also see a darker side, calling the Apache "lords of carnage" and "tawny killers."

The "water refrain" as part of "the woof and warp of the Southwest" forcefully applies to the cattlemen who followed them. The Apache needed water to survive; the ranchers needed it to harvest the land's "scant annuity" for grazing their cattle. Calvin once tips his hand regarding his feelings for ranchers when he observes that "it was not the cows but the cowmen" to whom he objected, although he does recognize the economic necessity of their pursuit. He can understand and admire the character of those who undertook it. For him ranching was "the combat of man and his beasts with nature," and "the magnitude of the adventure explains...the caliber of the men who ventured."

The "Sky Powers" were never far from Calvin's thinking though; rain was everything. Calvin offers this anecdote: "So it is not strange that in New Mexico when it rains, they say, 'What fine weather!'" He also reminds us that it is one of nature's ironies that often the best soil for growing grass is in the forest—not where cattle can easily access it, as they can in riparian habitat. The forest is the repository of stored moisture where it benefits neither agriculture nor grazing. So, in ranching, the difference "between success and failure...may consist in the utilization of a few varieties of humble bushes." To succeed, the stockman had better know what they are, where to find them, and what makes them so. The scientist in Calvin takes over as he answers those questions. Again though, water, as everywhere in arid country, is "paramount." There must be water, even if it must be drilled for, and then there must be a way to access it: "Nowhere is life so abundant and so jubilant as at the water's edge in the desert."

5

The Book's Reception

While *Sky Determines* obviously merited its warm reception, if for no other reason than its freshly articulated thesis, Macmillian's publicity department must have been hard at work as well from its offices in the epicenter of the big-city Eastern newspapers. Little remains of Calvin's reaction to the reviews, though he was never indifferent to them or to sales. Many years later, he voiced his pleasure when he described "the joy an author has when the reviews come pouring in from magazines and newspapers." In 1942 he informed a fan that the book was out of print but "every copy was sold at the original price" instead of being "tossed out" on the remainder bin. He added that there would not be a new edition because publication was "too much of a financial risk." There would, of course, be new editions published by the University of New Mexico in 1948 and 1965 and facsimile editions in 1993 and 2016 by others.

Justifiably, Calvin did take umbrage at one of the few totally negative reviews. In *The New Yorker* magazine's "Town Crier" column, Alexander Woollcott, renowned for his caustic manner, held that Calvin's book was "not all that might be desired." He went on, "The faults are in the literary quality.... [It is] rather lacking in penetration, satisfied frequently with superficial observation." That was a direct affront to Calvin the nature observer. He underlined the waspish clause alleging "superficial observation" and penned, "Did Mr. Alexander Woollcott know what he was talking about? Not much that he knew!"

Woollcott's was the only really negative review among many positively glowing ones that appeared. *The New York Times* conferred the prestige of a lengthy, front-page review in its book section, favorably comparing Calvin to eighteenth-century English parson-naturalist Gilbert White. Calling *Sky Determines* "a book of great charm," the review's author, R. L. Duffus, also drew favorable comparisons to Mary Austin's *The Land of Little Rain* (1903). He wrote that *Sky Determines* contains passages reflecting "qualities of beauty, even of spirituality." Duffus did, however, note that Calvin did not "insist," as Austin had, on the "subtler influences" of earth and sky to influence those who dwelled on and under them. Duffus continued in this vein when he added that Calvin's method of treating the Southwestern climate, flora, and fauna commends itself to White's ideas, because the approach to their subject "exists in the spirit of the two men." The reviewer for *The Republic* magazine had much the same impression, adding that Calvin "had informed" the theory of climatic foreordination with "a sensitiveness of his own."

The journal of the United Kingdom's Royal Geographical Society observed that the book's title is "a paraphrase" for climatic control. The lengthy, well-argued article did feel it a "serious defect" that some passages were "often florid and over-written." Both the Royal Geographic Society and the American Geographical Society predictably lamented the absence of maps. *The New York Herald Tribune* called *Sky Determines* an "authentic book," adding that it is "valuable as an introduction to a region of strange beauty and as an exposition of some little understood aspects of our history."

The most poignant of the reviews, because of its attendant circumstances, came from fellow New Mexico author Eugene Manlove Rhodes. W. H. Hutchinson recounts the story in *A Bar Cross Man: The Life & Personal Writings of Eugene Manlove Rhodes*. In the spring of 1934 Rhodes was ill and living in southern California, far from the scene of his masterpiece about the Land of Enchantment, *Pasó por aquí*. Despite his failing health, he reviewed *Sky Determines* for *The San Diego Union*; it was his last published piece. Rhodes mailed the clipping to Calvin along with a warm letter:

"Congratulations on *Sky Determines*. A charming book." Rhodes declared it the "only book that I have seen about New Mexico which admits that the world does not end suddenly just south of Albuquerque. Give us some more."

The day after the review's June 24 appearance, Rhodes suffered a severe attack of angina pectoris. This passed. On the following day, after posting the letter shortly before noon, Rhodes took to his bed, where he suffered a series of heart spasms. He died in the arms of his wife at dawn on the morning of June 27. Rhodes's letter accompanying the review was also his last. Written with a strong hand at the beginning, it diminishes to near illegibly near the end with the words, "Very sick. Excuse scrawl." It ends, "*Ave et vale*" (hail and farewell). Then, "Good luck." The letter's impact on Calvin was pronounced. A few days later he participated in a Fourth of July parade in Silver City. One newspaper reported that he tried to be cheerful but was "clearly downcast," thinking of Rhodes and his final missive.

Rhodes's review was chiefly laudatory with pronouncements such as this: "Calvin has written unpretentiously and eagerly of wonder and delight of the land he loves.... What he wrote with joy we may read with pleasure." Rhodes did feel constrained to note some "serious faults." If *Sky Determines* has a problem, he believed, it is its lack of original insight into the very nature of the state. Rhodes felt Calvin had not underscored enough "the kaleidoscopic character of beauty in this richest of all poor lands...that the bright high mountains of today will be dwindled and dim tomorrow, that the drab repulsive desert of one day will be magicked into the land of your dreams by the light of another sky. This also, 'Sky Determines.'" Thus the dying man seems to have foreseen a time when those attracted to New Mexico's essential character and beauty would foul their new nest and change it by the life-styles they brought with them, including too much reliance on too little water and polluting the night sky by too much artificial light.

New Mexico Magazine held simply that the importance of climate had "never been adequately developed" until *Sky Determines*. U.S. Weather Service lead forecaster and meteorologist David Hefner concurs. He believes climate weighs heavily on explaining civilization. The magazine added that Calvin offered "a novel viewpoint and a new approach" to looking at how weather impacts New Mexico and the Southwest.

Back home, the *Silver City Enterprise*, while lacking a book editor to produce a review of its own, nevertheless proudly printed a list of the newspapers and magazines around the country that had reviewed the book. Among those not already mentioned were the *Boston Transcript*, *Rocky Mountain News*, *Chicago Tribune*, *Los Angeles Times*, and *Albuquerque Journal*. The *Enterprise* also pitched in to promote sales. It offered $1.50 off the combined price of the book and a year's subscription if readers bought both at once. Nationally known New Mexico chronicler and famed Scripps Howard columnist Ernie Pyle gave *Sky Determines* a ringing endorsement: "practically our Southwestern Bible." He was later to become a friend of Calvin's. Meanwhile, a newspaper in neighboring Tombstone, Arizona, stirred itself only enough to call *Sky Determines* "an interesting book."

Even a sociological journal weighed in with Margaret Park Redfield commenting in *The American Journal of Sociology* that the book's theme could "be applied more adequately to the interpretation of Mother Nature than that of human nature." It is clever phrasing but not totally accurate. Calvin devoted as much space to the peoples who trod upon desert, mountains, and forests as he did to the physical landscape. Redfield further observed that the environment "determines the choices but does not determine the form which a culture will take." Surely she could not have been reading closely. When Calvin described the Puebleños slaying one of Coronado's Franciscan friars, "he fell to the ancestral deities and the religion of the rain." She lamented that the book focused on the study of the Navajo and Puebleños "in a conventionally enthusiastic way [but] does not contribute much to this interest." Like many other newcomers before him, Calvin was entranced by the native's ceremonies and life-styles; however, he did not even get into that until he had thoroughly examined the Pueblo people/white American interface and shown how the sky determines everything in these people's lives.

Sky Determines also sparked interest for a New Mexico college professor who was then surveying the state's literary landscape for a book he was writing. It is one of the few surviving contemporary pictures of Calvin the man, not just the priest or the writer. In July 1934, Dr. Lester Raines of the English Department at the New Mexico Normal University in Las Vegas traveled south to interview Calvin. What resulted was a first-hand description of Calvin at the prime of his life in his mid-forties along with the interviewer's impressions.

Raines was taken with the self-described "country parson" (who in reality was nothing of the sort). His descriptions of Calvin and his book are flowery, fawning, gushing. Regardless of its frequent hyperbole, Raines's account was the first extended interview with Calvin and the only one before Ernie Pyle's some five years later. Raines's interview yielded several interesting verbal snapshots of the subject. For example, Calvin said he had emerged from seminary as "a High Churchman." More importantly, Calvin shared how he wrote *Sky Determines*. This was not the only time he articulated the process, but it is one instance where he spelled out the steps most clearly:

> I drew on a file of 600 photographs which I made, labeled, and dated with great care. Then, too, I had a written record which afforded a detailed information on the flora, fauna, climatic data, ect, ect [*sic*] of the Southwest. The problem in writing the book in distinction from that of magazine articles was to examine a great mass of data, and figure out whither it pointed. All that remained was to marshal the facts into a thesis and then put it into respectable prose.

One important aid to Calvin's writing process, which he did not mention, was his use of note cards he carried with him everywhere.

Ross Calvin used index cards to supplement his field notations of observations for his Log Books; sometimes it was a sketch of plant life as shown here. (Ross Calvin Papers, Center for Southwest Research, University Libraries, University of New Mexico)

To treat "so imperial a theme" as *Sky Determines* with a style "stately yet compassionate and poignantly sincere calls for a man of no mean ability," Raines writes in *Writers and Writings of New Mexico* (1934).

Raines thought Calvin worthy of his attention and was a ready admirer. He pictures Calvin as "witty, jolly, kind and marvelously human." He depicts the author with "a personality that reaches out and gathers friends unto himself." Of *Sky Determines* he gushes, "And such a lot of facts, and such prose!" Conveying Calvin's description of the desert, he writes: "And we find it not unlovely, this place where the thorn yields its scepter and the barbs of Gehenna combine with the blossoms of Paradise." Raines says one of Calvin's friends told him, "The man must have absorbed his environment like a sponge." Raines rejects the easy cliché: "Rather to me," he responds in his inflated prose, Calvin "seems to have drunk it in as thirstily as his avid sands steal the moisture from the wandering clouds. And then has poured it forth again from the pages of his book in a clear, sparkling flood, slightly overwhelming in its immensity."

Raines carried away one other interesting impression from his interview. He writes that for Calvin poetry held no appeal (though Calvin did contribute one poem to a learned journal), but that he had "always longed to write prose, exquisite prose." Yet, Raines adds, "His book is filled with beautiful passages more poetic than any flowery verse." Raines quotes Calvin as saying that his inspiration for his writing was the "Master Classic," the Bible, and its "companion piece," The Book of Common Prayer.

6

The Book's Continuing Importance

Calvin would write many other works that can still appeal to present-day readers, but his continuing reputation stands, or falls, on *Sky Determines*, both for its scientific worth and for its literary value. How does it measure up today by either standard? Pretty well. Scientifically, it still receives high marks. True, meteorologist David Hefner has some reservations. He does not believe everything Calvin wrote about New Mexico weather was "entirely accurate," but it contains "kernels of truth," and so Calvin's ideas remain current "with a few semantic changes," as "we are still at the mercy of the weather elements."

"The lesson to take [away]," as fellow meteorologist David J. Novlan frames it, is that "we must still respect and study the sky." Should we care? "Certainly," says Hefner, as the two men play their thoughts back and forth. "The sky is not the only factor in our existence," observes Novlan, "but it still remains a dominant player." He himself "would start with the word *water*." He emphasizes the importance of the obvious: that "aridity after all" is the "lack of water." He also reminds us that "many people are starting to say—with the ongoing and possible continuing droughts, particularly in the West—[that] Water and not Oil is rapidly becoming the new gold."

Novlan points out significant differences eighty years

have brought. In the past, when there was no "technological enhancement" (wells, for example); one was totally dependent on the "sky" to provide water. Novlan interprets "sky" to mean climatology, the statistical sums, the means, the extremes of all continuous weather events, and a major influence on civilization and economics in general. With those parameters established, he believes Calvin had "a good handle" on his topic and that weather "influences our lives on a daily basis from cradle to grave." "We have a lot of technology to help protect us and adapt," says Novlan, "but the energy involved in weather systems is large and still dominates." Thus, he concludes, "Calvin's thesis is still valid...despite our advances in technology" which he believes "smart people" will utilize to optimize their safety and economic status.

Novlan further notes that the country's population density, as compared with eighty years ago when the book was written, "is starting to get in our way when we try to evacuate from hurricanes or get caught on freeways during a flash flood or blizzard." Novlan leaves us with this admonition: "People should still care and learn the following lesson: we are still vulnerable to the sky—or weather." He concludes that "like those who have gone before us we must still study and respect the sky—that is, climatology and meteorology—and not let modern technology lure us into a false sense of security. His parting shot is this: "There have been and will continue to be a lot of extreme weather events...thus...The Sky Determines!"

The importance of "sky" continues to draw attention. William deBuys in *The Walk* (2007) observes that "it is a sky that has shaped land and people not by what it gives but by what it does not have and therefore must withhold [water]...." New Mexico Black Range author, former research biologist, and outdoorsman Harley Shaw believes *Sky Determines* offers an "amazingly advanced [and] pretty accurate perception" of the effects of climate on New Mexico. He thinks the book underscores the role of "the Sky Powers" in determining climate and environment.

Despite his book's title, Calvin displays a certain fondness for mountains. He notes that New Mexico's Canadian and Alpine summits "store the water for the thirsty lands below them." What a pertinent observation—mountains as reservoir, just waiting until they are called on to play their role. It is an "intelligent and providential thing" he observes about the moisture, in that it lies there waiting until needed—usually in June, often New Mexico's hottest month. Snowmelts, which all New Mexicans eagerly look forward to each year, and summer rains seem to work "in concert," as one offsets the other, to ensure a sufficient supply of moisture. This causal relationship is another example of Calvin's keen eye.

Calvin discusses the unevenness of rainfall distribution and its effects on the "myriads of life forms." He explains that a rise in altitude produces a drop in temperature and that a drop in temperature causes an increase in rainfall. Although rainfall varies in New Mexico, Mary Austin is right: New Mexico is indeed *The Land of Little Rain*. Calvin discusses the types of vegetation that grow in response to rainfall they do or do not receive: mesquite, creosote bush, and cacti. "Mesquite still carries on, even after the cacti have dropped out of the race."

Calvin tells the reader of the "markers" for the various zones and their vegetative and animal characteristics. He notes a clear demarcation of Lower and Upper Sonoran Zones at Silver City, the area of New Mexico he knew best. For Calvin there was much to like in the natural world. Coyotes, despised by ranchers, are "nature's trickiest, full-size sneakers." They take as food whatever comes their way; they are survivors. The prickly pear might be considered their vegetative counterpart. "I devour, I devoured, I am devoured" could be words to live by. How can the reader not relate to his concept? "The thorn was doubtless nature's first weapon," he muses. He notes with admiration that "the cactus flies the gaudiest flag in a land where nature uses color without stint...."

What really sets *Sky Determines* apart, which some critics at the time noted, is its interpretation of New Mexico and the Southwest. Several earlier writers, including John Van Dyke in *The Desert* (1901), Walter Prescott Webb in *The Great Plains* (1931), and John Wesley Powell in the late nineteenth century, had written with affection and insight about the area. But they did not provide the equivalent of Calvin's commentary on the climatic impact. Here Calvin is at his best as he explains how the "Sky Powers" affects the nonhuman entities of desert, mountains, and forests, as well as those beings that inhabit them. Calvin knew *Sky Determines* is a "fresh and permanent" approach to the Southwest and "a new and creative interpretation" of its life.

The matter of interpretation, a word that is part of the book's subtitle, is an interesting concept to consider. Many years later, Calvin attempted to explain what he meant by the term and the role he thought an interpreter performed. The question to consider, he posits, is why an affair turns out one way rather than another. "First," he writes, "he [the interpreter] concentrates... on explanation rather than on narration." After that, he continues, "he considers first its history, then the contemporary scene, tries to read portents of the future, calculates trends, examines old failures, ponders significance, summarizes, reflects, deduces—and finally guesses." In 1965 he confessed to *New Mexico Quarterly* readers that his "worse guesses" related to "two facts which no man could then foresee"—the phenomenal growth of Albuquerque and the detonation of the atomic bomb. (These two occurrences were fresh in his mind, having visited them in the third edition of *Sky Determines*.)

In addition to offering interpretation, another "ulterior purpose" Calvin claimed for his book, an ambitious social one, was to lift mankind—then facing worldwide economic uncertainties and threats—to peace. He wanted his readers to recognize that nature had an answer: "in the world of roots and clouds and wings and leaves there exists no Depression."

There may be no one more qualified to speak on the lasting impact of *Sky Determines* and Calvin's contributions to Southwestern literature than science and naturalist writer Sharman Apt Russell. Her essays have been widely anthologized and translated, and her work has garnered numerous awards. When this "back to the lander" calls *Sky Determines* a "seminal work," be assured it is just that. Fresh out of graduate school, Russell and her husband, Peter, wanted "to root into the land, to sink into the soil and sun." One of the books that reinforced their decision to seek a fresh start in New Mexico's rural Mimbres Valley was *Sky Determines*. They read everything they could find about "this new place" they had decided to call home. For them Calvin's work places the history and people of New Mexico in the "context of earth and sky, animals and plants." It helped them understand the natural world that "stood at the center" of the Southwest. Some three and a half decades after they first read it, the book's message still resonates with them, "still makes sense." Russell says Calvin's view of "what determines" seems even "more pertinent today" in the face of climate change and an increasingly arid Southwest. She is convinced the sun and sky will play "an even greater role" in how humans exercise their stewardship. She believes country dwellers like her have a continued role to play as neighbors and protectors of the public lands that make up so much of New Mexico: "We remain at the interface of what is wild and what is not, sustained by a personal relationship to this landscape."

Allyson Siwik is another transplanted Easterner who moved to New Mexico because of Calvin's message. In visiting New Mexico some twenty years ago with her soon-to-be husband, Dennis O'Keefe, she found it difficult to make sense of a landscape so wildly different from her native Connecticut as well as Maine and North Carolina, where she attended college. In New Mexico, she found, "one could see for miles across huge expanses of land blanketed by grassland and dotted with small trees." In many places, "the bones of the earth" seem "exposed from weathering from wind, sun, and rain. Wild fire had left behind blackened snags.... Cactus and ponderosa pine would appear virtually side by side." A biologist by training, Siwik found herself fascinated by what she saw and yearning to learn more.

O'Keefe had given her a copy of *Sky Determines* early in their relationship. It was that to which she now turned. "What a joy [the book] was to dig into," she recalls, "providing me with the understanding to read our landscape with a keen eye to the forces—both natural and man-made—that shaped our environment." Siwik now finds herself protecting Calvin Country as the director of the Gila Resources Information Project. She wonders how the Southwestern landscape will change as global climate change brings hotter, drier conditions. The Gila National Forest, for example, has already seen high-intensity wildfire and associated flooding that has changed the path of the river. How can we adapt, Siwik asks, without making the mistakes of the past? "*Sky Determines*," she believes, "helps us to understand these forces in an accessible and interesting manner to layperson and scientist alike."

Jim Norwine, author of more than fifty scholarly articles and ten books, including *The Changing Climate of Texas* (1998) and *A World After Climate Change and Culture-Shift* (2013), thinks Calvin's view is "romantic, almost metaphysical." He feels *Sky Determines* employs a literary, yet "very accessible," style. Norwine sees the book as an "objective/subjective hybrid." On the one hand, he believes it to be a scientific explanation of a climate-driven landscape and, on the other, "a kind of love letter to that landscape."

While Tom Hester would not elevate Calvin to the level of Henry David Thoreau or John Wesley Powell, he does believe Calvin's "ambition" to explain New Mexico in terms of climatic impact and then being able to relate it to culture and economics is "startling for his time" and "[i]n these days of calculating solar resources, more startling still." Hester believes Calvin was a man of exquisite observations and big ideas ahead of their time. Hester has done a lot of thinking about Calvin, even teaching a course on him. For it, he provided a series of questions for his students to wrestle with. Would Calvin have written *Sky Determines* had he lived in a small town in Nebraska or Missouri? If so, would it have been as good as *Sky Determines*? If Calvin had lived in Taos, how would have *Sky Determines* been different?

Hester himself thinks *Sky Determines* would have been different had Calvin lived in Taos, but his answer is not the obvious one. Hester believes it has to do with landscape. Silver City was more of a desert environment in Calvin's time than Taos, he explains. "Calvin had more of an impression of the sky in Silver City then than today," he says. "Landscape determines the writer.... [T]hey were two different landscapes." Further, Taos has long been an arts community, unlike Silver City until only recently. Hester understands that a necessary quality for an environmental writer is the ability to see the big picture but to be able to focus on and see the detail in microscopic events as well. Calvin was able to look at the larger scene and then "drill down."

Silver City author, publisher, and outdoorsman M. L. "Dutch" Salmon values both the book's "conservation ethic" and its "elegant and literate" tone. He quotes Calvin himself: "Crowding is bad for the body of man.... It is worse for the spirit of man." Calvin thought that in New Mexico, people "will never be crowded—crowded and thus crushed. There are cities enough elsewhere." Calvin predicted the state would experience a growth spurt. "[I]t is fair to say that the flowing of waters...banished the former curses of isolation, backwardness, chronic poverty. The despot sky no longer determines. There will certainly rise no metropolitan cities...." Albuquerque proved him wrong. Calvin, however, would still argue that the state's essential character remains: "But the mountains that billow starkly against the sunset will not change. The high, thin purity of the air will not change, and the holy sunshine will not change." Salmon so admires Calvin and *Sky Determines* and its message that in

1993 his High-Lonesome Books brought out a paperback edition of the 1948 University of New Mexico edition. It was "quite natural," Salmon explained, for his press—situated as it is in the southwestern part of the state—to want *Sky Determines*, "the best known book to emanate from that region," back in print.

7

Lawrence Clark Powell, A Special Bond

Lawrence Clark Powell about 1960 in his office at the library at the University of California, Los Angeles (UCLA) (Leo Linder, Academic Communications, Facility, UCLA)

Lawrence Clark Powell's treatment of *Sky Determines* years later in his own books was different from that of reviewers and meteorologists and an equally gratifying form of recognition. As librarian, critic, bibliophile, or author, there simply was no regional man of letters of Powell's stature. So when he called *Sky*

Determines a classic, which he did many times, it was the highest possible praise. Powell was a longtime librarian at UCLA and later professor-in-residence at the University of Arizona. From those positions he observed and wrote lovingly of his Southwest and its literature.

With Powell's nod of approval, the continuing place of *Sky Determines* in the Southwestern canon was assured. Powell included it in a series of reassessments of Southwestern literature published in *Westways* magazine between 1971 and 1972. These and other reappraisals were later collected in his aptly titled *Southwest Classics* (1974), a volume of essays on the people, landscape, and literature of the Southwestern arid lands he considered classics. In addition to Calvin, his book included sketches of such well known chroniclers of the region as D. H. Lawrence, Mary Austin, Willa Cather, Erna Fergusson, Eugene Manlove Rhodes, Oliver LaFarge, Joseph Wood Krutch, and J. Frank Dobie. As Powell put it, "In books, and memorably in these of my choice, we see one southwest refracted through many prisms."

Tarleton State University English professor William T. Pilkington, who also wrote widely on Southwestern literature, observed in his *My Blood's Country: Studies in Southwestern Literature* (1973) that Powell's goal in profiling these authors was "the illumination of quality rather than the accumulation of quantity." Pilkington held that Powell demonstrated a bibliophile's "unerring instinct" for discovering and making known those works that were "indispensable" to understanding the region.

Powell wrote of Calvin and *Sky Determines* several times over the course of nearly two decades. In *Southwestern Book Trails* (1982), he expanded on his original thought in *Southwestern Classics* to comment that *Sky Determines* was "central in New Mexico literature." He further noted that "among the vast number of books about the Southwest, proliferating endlessly, classics are few. That in his good long life of eighty years, [if] Ross Calvin achieved one and only one…only one is needed to place an author in our pantheon." As adumbrated in this comment, Powell was later to view the book as essentially a one-off effort, with Calvin having no more good books in him after his initial success. Several years earlier, Calvin himself seemed to agree. In late March 1949 he wrote Lyle Saunders at the University of Texas that "probably I'll never do anything again as good" as *Sky Determines*." He went on, however, to say that what other success his writing may have had, "here's an achievement that really came through."

Like Eugene Manlove Rhodes before him, Powell credited Calvin for rescuing southwestern New Mexico from a literary dark hole and bringing the region into the light of awareness. Writing that "literature in New Mexico previously had flourished best in the upper reaches [of the state]...from Albuquerque through Santa Fe to Taos," Powell noted that the southeastern section had "few laureates" save for Rhodes and Paul Horgan; it had "languished in a literary sense" until Calvin came along. Powell felt that Calvin's Plains upbringing and his exposure to the world around him in Illinois heightened his "ability precisely to see and to interpret nature." His literary and linguistic studies enhanced his power of description. All this, Powell noted, was brought to bear on showcasing the "enthralling new environment" Calvin discovered upon his arrival in New Mexico.

All these compliments created a special bond between the two, though perhaps more so on Calvin's part. In writing the editor of *Westways* to propose an article, Calvin wrote that Powell "calls my *Sky Determines* 'the finest single article about New Mexico,'" rating it "the best of all advertisements for the Land of Enchantment."

The 1965 University of New Mexico Press edition of *Sky Determines* illustrated by Peter Hurd. (University of New Mexico Press)

He voiced his appreciation directly to Powell. A year later, just before another reprinting was scheduled, he wrote saying that "for many years you've been saying nice things about *Sky Determines*, but the last time was the one that brought down the apple!" In the spring of 1965, with the second University of New Mexico Press edition of *Sky Determines* about to appear, Calvin wrote, saying the "book will be out about June—and the first one will be yours." Had he known what Powell was to write of it, he might have restrained himself.

With the last edition of *Sky Determines* Powell was unhappy. He understood that Calvin and the University of New Mexico had tried to build on the beauty and grace of the 1934 edition by adding seventy-four pages of material showing that New Mexico *had* changed in the thirty-one intervening years between printings because of the detonation of the atomic bomb at Trinity Site and the state's accompanying explosive growth in population. But he felt they had missed the mark. Commenting that what was called for was a new and separate book instead of a reprint of the 1948 edition, he wrote:

> Unable to achieve this, he succeeded only in blemishing his earlier work. There was no one to save the book from its author, and from the desire of the publisher to make it an up-to-date work on the state. It would seem that its first brilliant success had dazzled Ross Calvin. Lost was the gift of self-criticism. His power over language had weakened. He was unable to recognize that he had in him only a single inspiration which came at the summit of his prime and which never came again.

Although there is no record of it, Calvin must have felt wounded, especially since he had worked so hard for a reissue, wondering why the book has ever been allowed to go out of print in the first place. Ironically, in lobbying to make his case, he told University of New Mexico president Tom Popejoy that those whose opinions counted—notably long-time advocate Lawrence Clark Powell—felt a new edition was needed. He even said Powell had voiced an "insistence" on a new edition.

8

Church Tensions

Almost from the beginning Calvin contemplated a sequel to *Sky Determines*. Given its success, it is difficult to understand why the follow-up project did not materialize as contemplated. It was, however, still the Depression, and money was hard to come by. We know his intentions, his thoughts for what broad areas the book would cover, and even its working title. This comes from his reply to an information request from the *Biographical Directory of American Men of Science*. He gave its title as *Arid Centuries* and claimed the book was "nearing completion" (a refrain he was to repeat frequently). Professor Moses supplies a more complete title: *Arid Centuries: Man's Impact on Nature in the Southwest*. Intended as a continuation of *Sky Determines*, it was to examine the effect of various cultures on the arid environment with special attention to erosion, an issue in which he was becoming increasingly interested, along with deterioration of plant life and associated matters. The concept in essence was simply turning the tables on the ideas expressed in *Sky Determines*, which had examined the effect of aridity on Southwestern cultures.

Never reticent about the value of the proposed sequel, Calvin said it was pioneering in "a real sense" but not easily classified. The studies, he said, "lie in between the physical and the social sciences." Calvin sent the manuscript to Macmillan in early 1937. He noted in his private journal that "a load has been lifted from my shoulders." Soon after this came another entry: "Bad news from Macmillan." However, he did not give up. He again reported to friends that the book was still "nearing completion." The title, however, had changed to *Portrait of the Southwest*. It was not until nearly ten years later that the book was published, and then only after major revisions and a totally different title: *River of the Sun: Stories of the Storied Gila River*.

He continued to pen articles. Two of the most interesting from this period relate his abiding interest in science. In "Approach to the Temple of Science," Calvin described his scientific growth as something he could no longer call a hobby: "Having learned the names of hundreds of plants, we at length passed beyond the stage where we could be satisfied with mere names." Field study, where all about him was an abundance of opportunity, led to understanding the distribution of plants. From there, it was a natural progression to comprehending their competition for water, sunshine, and nutrients and then to "natural groupings into societies having similar needs and preferences." This insight led to his seeing the relationship between certain plants and certain rocks and soils. The acquisition of a microscope, somehow bought on a parson's meager salary, enabled him to see the structure of plants and the way they grew. That led to wanting to know how they were recorded in fossils, which he could see everywhere he trod. Finally, when personal observation left him wanting, he turned to the written word in journals and scholarly tomes for further knowledge.

One *New Mexico Magazine* piece in 1939 was ecological in nature, while still another dealt with the state's resources and how best to use them. "Fire in the Trees" recalled a forest fire in New Mexico's Black Range on June 15, 1938, on nearly the same day as a later one in 2013 and very near the same spot. After noting the ways in which a forest can die naturally, Calvin observes that "when death and ruin come...by means of man-caused fire, that is very different. We feel the keenest sort of resentment.... [E]verybody loses...." He concludes that regrowth "is a race between the constructive and destructive forces of nature." Calvin voices the hope that "green leaves will gain the decision over sterility and desolation." Foresters read his article yet today.

Meanwhile, some of his flock was beginning to think he spent too much time at his typewriter and not enough with them. For them, this might have been expressed as too much pen and not enough pulpit. Then he got into a spot of bother with his superior for allegedly entertaining the possibility of taking a new assignment in Phoenix. The two issues became connected since, for Bishop Howden, Phoenix represented just another way of providing Calvin more time to indulge his writing passion to the exclusion of his priestly duties. Part of the problem was of Calvin's own making. He responded to a "long and persuasive" letter that a church in Phoenix was his "for the writing." That, at least, was how Calvin put it when Howden learned of the situation.

Calvin felt compelled to defend himself. In a series of letters to the bishop in late 1937, Calvin wrote that he wanted to be "completely clear" that his writing was not done "on time stolen from my ministry." Calvin pointed out that he studied and wrote in his leisure time "while many other men amuse themselves with cards, light novels, etc. etc." He always eschewed such pursuits, denouncing them as wasted time. Calvin displayed occasional asperity when Howden remarked on Calvin's time spent writing and what the bishop saw as his priest's time away from Good Shepherd duties. His response was sharply worded and to the point. "I do my work," he asserted, "and an amount of it that challenges comparison." Calvin often felt constrained to show how hard he worked. In fairness, he did. All that may have taken a toll on him and explains his occasional acerbity and inability to relate to his family or others. He did not suffer fools gladly, even when they might be his bishop. He left this parting shot. "Then if there is any time, I do my writing." He further observed that "although fatigue brings on insomnia...I have missed but two Sundays in ten years by reason of illness."

Howden's "personal opinion" was that Calvin should "seriously consider" any opportunity of going to Phoenix. "In connection with your writing," he continued, "I am inclined to feel that a more circumscribed work [such as in Phoenix] would fit in better with your allotment of time." The word "allotment" set Calvin off. He was indignant. Calvin told his boss he had not gone to Arizona to seek another church. He remained in Silver City until his eventual transfer to Clovis.

Another exchange of letters occurred when another priest showed interest in snagging Calvin's job at Good Shepherd. The would-be poacher informed Howden he thought Calvin was "in a somewhat depleted nervous condition and that Mrs. Calvin was also far from well." The nature of Grace's illness was left unstated but the inference was clear enough. Those observations about the couple's health likely had some basis in fact. Calvin was overworked, perhaps overwrought. Grace may have begun showing signs of the illness that would later claim her. Calvin confronted this poaching issue head on. "It is strange what curious misinformation about me often reaches you," he told Howden, leaving him to "wonder about its source." Calvin said he was left to "conclude that if the Rev. Mr. — is a friend of mine, he is not a very straightforward friend. A man scheming to supplant another in his work—well, that speaks for itself."

Yet another issue between Calvin and Howden concerned the growth of Good Shepherd and St. Luke's in Deming, where Calvin was also responsible. Calvin informed his superior that the "building up" of Good Shepherd was being done "all the time, steadily and at a reasonable rate." He doubted anyone could do better. Calvin pointed out that 1936 was the most successful of his ten years in Silver City, with improved attendance, a functioning choir, a large Sunday school, and an improved physical plant. These were measurable yardsticks few could argue with. "But at Deming the case is very different," he conceded. Only later could he write that the church there had finally "turned the corner."

Difficulties between rector and bishop continued. Calvin felt he had to defend his time ministering to prisoners and the money he spent on their reading matter. This issue surfaced in a letter to the bishop from the diocese's women's reading society. Calvin, more interested in the incarcerated than in women's circles, risked the bishop's ire by saying that the funds would do "a great deal of useful service" in providing reading material for the imprisoned rather than for the women of the church. "The latter have more periodicals than they can read," he shot back. "Not so the prisoners. They can buy nothing for themselves, and consequently they read stale newspapers and pulp magazines." This view did not go down well with the bishop.

Calvin had a stubborn side, and here he was unwavering. He tried one more time to win over the bishop to his way of thinking. "I am convinced

[my] hours spent among prisoners are far more effective in lasting results than an equal time spent among students, health-seekers or any other extra-parochial group whatsoever. Where all kindness is so rare," he tried to explain, "any little act of kindness is valued high." He recalled standing beside a wife as her husband appeared before the bench to receive his sentence. Since then, Calvin told his bishop, "No Christmas has passed without a card" from them. Or a man on trial reading from cover to cover a New Testament Calvin had given him. He had also intervened for a CCC worker who had run afoul of the law. He called such ministry "more fruitful" and thus bringing him "more happiness than any mission work I have done since."

These observations were offset by a postscript in which he told Howden that the past summer had brought "some misfortunes" to the family." He reported being tortured for weeks with "the old trouble" of insomnia and said that Grace had to have two months' "rest" in the sanatorium. This is the earliest surviving reference to her illness and need for treatment. Whatever Grace's illness was, it could sometimes be frightening for her as well as for those around her. Rodney recounted to his son one occasion from Silver City days in which he watched helplessly as his mother tried to cook eggs over the kitchen stove when her arms suddenly began jerking uncontrollably. She finally threw the skillet across the room in frustration. Her condition was not to improve.

Calvin continued to strongly defend his work with the imprisoned. He again laid out his thoughts in a 1938 article for the church's *The Spirit of Missions*. His title came from Matthew 25:43. "In Prison, And Ye Visited Me Not!" He hoped the subheading of his article, "Rise in crime demands that Church do what must be done and faithfully heed the Master's command," would inspire his fellow clergy to follow Christ's teaching and Calvin's own example. He began by asking, "I wonder how many clergy ever once spoke to a criminal calling him by name, or ever once talked to him as man to man?" It is past time to do so, he declared. Calvin did admit that "prisoners, next to relief clients, are probably the world's greatest complainers...." Lest a visiting priest allow himself to be taken in by a prisoner's tale of woe, Calvin offered this: "The visitor must be, while harmless as a dove, as wise as a serpent."

He cautioned that inmates were wary of "professional brotherly love" but that they responded to genuine manly affection and care. Calvin said he thought Christ "wants us to be neither soft-hearted nor hard-boiled—but both" in dealing with the incarcerated. He posed another question: what can a clergyman hope to achieve with his visits to the Grant County Jail? The first possibility as Calvin saw it is to "leave the prisoner convinced beyond the shadow of a doubt that he [the clergyman] comes as a friend" because a priest "cannot be shocked by anything that men and women do." In a prison, Calvin warned, the chaplain is looking into the "darkest abyss in the world" and into "a heart in which has died all hope in man and God." A second possible outcome is to convince the prisoner that crime is a mistake. Calvin spent no time exploring rehabilitation or recidivism, but he left his readers with this consideration: "It is not necessary to wait until the organist or senior warden is locked up...." He suggested that his fellow clergy "visit a cell sometime and stand awhile before whatever unhappy face is at the moment pressed against their bars of steel." He warned them not to be "too professionally pious." All this could have been a lecture at a religious conference; it is one of his finest pieces of writing for its forthrightness, honesty, and clarity.

Howden was unmoved, either by letters or articles. "I have no doubt that, personally members of the clergy are very kind in their intentions, especially in their individual personal relations with the under-dog," he responded. The standoff did not end. "[As] deserving of admiration as this is, the particular matter I am interested in" was the work of the Church Periodical Club. "All it needs is some cooperation." Howden was referring to Calvin's cooperation; he did not get it.

It was an inexorable rolling stream of problems from which Calvin could not easily extricate himself. Expenses were still another matter, and in a time when literally every dime counted, Calvin continued to seek every last cent of legitimate reimbursement he felt due him. Such efforts later got him into trouble with his church treasurer. Calvin reported having his car sideswiped after he had been called out on a snowy day to administer Holy Communion to a man who lay near death in a nearby town. Calvin asked his bishop to consider the "fairness of my claim" for the extra trip to administer the sacraments. Howden eventually paid both the repair bill and mileage, but only reluctantly. The bishop apparently had his eye on the bottom line, not on whether the injured man might leave this life without anointment of the dying.

Even innocent occurrences could attract envy and exacerbate a deteriorating situation. Such may well have occurred as a result of admiring attention paid Calvin in a widely popular nationally syndicated column in late 1939 by the famous future war correspondent Ernie Pyle. The article ran in *The Albuquerque Tribune* and the *El Paso Herald Post* (and around the country), so it was certainly seen and commented on in Silver City. It was a flattering picture but revealed a long-standing medical issue many knew nothing of. Calvin was then nearly forty-nine, "tall and slender" and "handsome and youngish." Pyle pictured him in a gray business suit and clerical collar, the kind worn by "almost [every] dashing young rector you read about in English novels." Further, he wrote, Calvin was "a bundle of action" with a "vim that finally winds him up into a knot of taut nerves." All that, Pyle said, led Calvin to "a dreadful insomnia," so that the clergyman "goes for weeks with almost no sleep at all." The newspaperman speculated that "a form of...nervousness" lay behind the insomnia. Calvin had endured the condition for fifteen years. In his "Minor Memorenda" [sic] twenty years later, Calvin noted the onset of the dreadful sleep disorder as occurring on March 19, 1929, and running through June 5, 1944.

Pyle told his readers he had intentionally left the "best part" about Calvin until last. That was where the minister hailed from—Chrisman, Illinois, ten miles west of that "well-known metropolis of Dana, Ind.," which had also produced "a man who is exceptionally good and brave and learned," a jocular self-effacing description of Pyle himself. "You just can't get ahead of us prairie boys," the columnist concluded. The Calvins treasured a personal souvenir of Pyle's visit—a photo dated November 9, 1939, of Pyle and his wife Gerry as they posed with their signature coupe in which they roamed the country seeking out material for his columns.

Calvin had duties beyond Good Shepherd and the mission church in Deming. He was also a conscientious, if somewhat testy, editor of the diocesan newsletter. A problem arose when Howden wrote Calvin that a priest had complained about the alleged vagueness and confused wording of a notice in the newsletter over postponement of the annual convocation. Calvin, with a PhD in philology from Harvard, was being challenged. He shot back. "There is no lack of definiteness in the notice.... If a man neglects to read a notice that concerns him," he continued, "there is nothing we can do about it."

That was minor. Larger problems loomed for Calvin at his own church. He had now been at Good Shepherd some fifteen years, and issues were bound to surface during a tenure of that duration. They became, however, a serious consideration regarding his continued presence there. Calvin continued to carry on a regular correspondence with his superior. A good deal dealt with administrative matters, both at Good Shepherd and within the diocese, in carrying out his various offices. A news release Calvin wrote for *Southwest Churchman* years later noted some of the diocesan offices he now held: newsletter editor, examining chaplain, member of the Council of Advice, and member of the Executive Council, among others. Calvin's letters began to take on a defensive tone. Some centered on the distaff side of the Good Shepherd congregation. During these exchanges, Howden exhibited his typical good will and understanding of Calvin's plight as one who most likely preferred to dwell in the realm of the mind rather than the temporal.

Calvin's apparent inability to understand and get along with some of the women in his parish particularly dogged him. In early October 1940, Calvin wrote Howden of his perplexity with a certain "Mrs. B—. Just what her grievance is, I am at a loss to say." Calvin assured his bishop that he had "not harmed her, and on the contrary have tried my level best to make peace." He went on to add, in his patriarchal fashion, "Of course, you can't fight a woman...." Calvin wanted to recognize the woman for her years of faithful service to Good Shepherd, "yet after she has become a Fifth Column [a term that came into vogue during the Spanish Civil War to refer to anyone attempting to undermine a larger group from within]—and I mean just that—it is only the part of wisdom to protect the work [of the church] against her harm." Then there was a certain "Mrs. M— whose dinner you will remember." He added that "it amazes me to see what little things excite and antagonize us all." It is not clear why Calvin referred to his female nemeses only by the initials of their last names.

The issue of expenses seemed never to go away. Mrs. B— was the parish treasurer, a bishopric appointment. Calvin wondered to Howden if she had "a more or less permanent hold on it?" Calvin felt the source of her animosity stemmed from her belief that he had collected too much on salary claims to which he was not entitled. He later returned the June grant, $25, which apparently had been in question. The misunderstanding arose from a very serious car accident the previous summer involving his family. A rear tire blew out on their automobile in the blistering June heat near Indio in the California desert, causing the vehicle to overturn twice. Calvin was thrown roughly to the highway when a door was ripped off. Calvin told the bishop that since then Mrs. B— "has made her hostility sharply felt."

His grievance is easily understood since the entire family was fortunate to have survived. All were injured, Calvin the most severely. He was so distraught that he later wrote a detailed two-page letter to General Motors, makers of the Chevrolet in which they had been riding, to explain why he felt the car's design and manufacture may have contributed to the accident. GM was not impressed enough to respond, let alone recompense the irate priest. He wrote yet another similar letter and sent carbon copies to several friends. He added a hand-written postscript to these, saying that "the car was a total wreck and me just about ditto!"

Because of the severity of his injury and the needed time to recuperate, Calvin overstayed his vacation leave. Grace wrote Howden from the hospital at Indio, where she remained with Calvin, "God only knows how we escaped being killed." Calvin sustained a skull fracture behind the ear and Peggy a broken arm. Howden was moved to offer to drive from Albuquerque to Indio to bring the family back home. They declined.

There were to be further consequences of the injury. Calvin was with Howden in Deming a year later when he experienced severe dizziness. He was hospitalized overnight. The attending physician told them both that he was "suspicious" of a connection with the California accident and ordered Calvin to rest for a few days and "take it easy." Calvin said that was "impossible." Howden concurred with the physician. "I feel quite sure that your doctor is right in ordering you to go slowly after such an experience...." There is no evidence that Calvin took it easy. If he ever did take off a day, it was more likely at his typewriter, not in his easy chair by the big Philco floor model radio the family enjoyed listening to as they heard Edward R. Murrow reporting from Europe on Hitler and America's possible involvement in war.

The deteriorating state of his relations with some members of the parish increased. He concluded one letter to Howden with "a good deal of regret" at having to write "with the full consciousness of my own faults." Calvin did not often indulge in any form of mea culpa. Now he expressed understanding why things "turn people against us from time to time." He was writing specifically of his dealings with Mrs. B—, but they might well have applied to a larger audience. Howden did not deal with the problems. He was good at confronting the ladies' reading group issues, but not so good with sensitive personnel issues posed by his touchy star priest. Besides, the bishop was in Albuquerque; Calvin's problems and his detractors were in Silver City.

Calvin's contentious relationship with some in the parish and with the vestry, however, finally demanded bishopric involvement, though not Howden's. That venerable shepherd died suddenly and unexpectedly on November 12, 1940, of a heart attack in Albuquerque at age seventy. It was a shock to Calvin. A note in his newspaper column three days later informed readers he was driving to Albuquerque at once to "do the last honor of friendship and respect." Four days later, Calvin wrote he had suggested a wreath of oak leaves for the bishop's funeral because Howden was "a man of oak, proved well-seasoned, sturdy oak." Calvin went beyond that with a warm, heartfelt tribute in a November 19 "Parson" column, noting that his late bishop, "in the midst of a blatant modernity...held firmly to the traditional ideals of the past." These beliefs, of course, were Calvin's as well. They were rooted in his education at Harvard with its long-standing traditions and in his study of seventeenth-century poets. Howden's ideas he too admired. Calvin wrote that while Howden was "a patrician," he never "treated anyone with condescension." Howden, he added, held his "own firmly-held ideals of dignity, fitness, [and] order," and "he looked ahead with faith." These were unconscious pronouncements on Calvin's own character.

Howden's death, in effect, settled the matter of Calvin's continued pastoral presence at Good Shepherd. It took almost a year for the interim bishop, Frederick B. Bartlett, to react, and he then acted decisively. In late October 1941, he drove down to Silver City from Albuquerque to preside over the confirmation of new church members. In meetings that followed the ceremonies, Bartlett quickly discerned the problem. "It did not take me long to catch the situation," he wrote Calvin upon returning to Albuquerque. "[There] was something in the air." Acting upon the belief that it was best to address the problem sooner rather than later, Bartlett wrote Calvin on October 29, offering him a new posting in Idaho, where he had been bishop and still had contacts. A day later he suggested another possibility "which you might find more attractive." It was still in New Mexico but on the other side of the state—in Clovis. Bartlett requested Calvin come to Albuquerque on November 1 to talk things over. To soften the blow, Bartlett offered a few diplomatic words: "Since you have faced these difficulties [Calvin later termed them "parish quarrels"] during the long period of fourteen years, I believe you should move to another *field* [Episcopal speak for a new posting]." Bartlett told Calvin he was entitled to a reasonable salary and "more peace of mind." The "reasonable salary" was $1800 a year.

Bartlett further sweetened the kitty with the promise of a new rectory, a $25 monthly travel allowance, and the possibility of teaching at Eastern New Mexico College in nearby Portales. The new posting, though it could be viewed as a forced transfer, was not necessarily an indictment of Calvin—just a recognition of the frictions that sometimes surface in pastor-parish relationships over time. The Clovis assignment was to begin in early 1942, so Calvin had little time to absorb the news and prepare for the move. There is no record of how much he mulled over his decision or hours spent in prayer or in discussion with Grace. In a way, Calvin had been outmaneuvered and given very little, if any, choice. Off he was to go to the windy high plains, away from his beloved mountains where the "Sky Powers" reigned and where he had found health, fame, and friendships.

Calvin had spent fifteen years in Silver City; his transfer was brought about in less than two weeks. Ironically, Bartlett was killed in an automobile accident in Idaho shortly after giving Calvin his new job. Calvin informed his *Daily Press* readers of the impending move to Clovis with a December 15, 1941, column headed "The Final Blessing." It began, "At last a letter from the Bishop-elect gives the green Go-signal [for the transfer]." Calvin suggested that if Silver City friends wanted to say good-bye there was no better time or place than at the eleven o'clock services on his final Sunday. "After that," he wrote, "the address will be Clovis, New Mexico—also a good town." When Calvin left Silver City, he likened the moving van taking his family's household goods to his new assignment unto "a hearse." Calvin did not know he was to have yet more productive writing success ahead of him in Clovis.

9

To the Plains: The Clovis Years

Little is known of Calvin's initial impression of his new home on New Mexico's high plains, or of his reception there, for that matter. His new hometown did not remotely resemble Silver City. That town, which he had once described as "one of the obscurest posts in the Church," he had come to love. Clovis is a mere nine miles west of Texico, a hamlet straddling the New Mexico-Texas state line. Gone are the mountains and vistas of wide open terrain to the west to be replaced by flat plains and fenced-in cotton and grain fields watered by the vast Ogallala Aquifer. Calvin early described the area as "windy [and] uninteresting." But it is more than that; it is the setting of a more conservative people both politically and religiously. The entire eastern side of New Mexico in which Calvin suddenly found himself has often been called "Little Texas." Where was his muse for writing? What could this landscape say to him? Even his religious work initially seemed unsatisfying. Despite all this, Calvin was ultimately to find as much creative satisfaction in Clovis as in Silver City. He was also to be instrumental in building a beautiful church that still today draws praise and admiration.

It took some time for him to adjust. Almost a year to the day after he had begun his new assignment, Calvin wrote J. C. Galbraith, an influential layman at the prestigious St. Clements

Church in El Paso who was closely involved in choosing a new rector. In this letter Calvin revealed a dimension of his religiosity and spirituality he did not often disclose in writing: "If I have any special gift in the sacred ministry, it would be...the preaching of personal religion." He began the letter like any typical job applicant. Noting that he was aware there were many highly qualified candidates, Calvin said he could "justify his place." He told Galbraith "not one [of his rivals]" had "a finer education" or "better training," and he continued by extolling his various virtues, not failing to mention his authorship of *Sky Determines*. St. Clements was a plum posting—one of two big parishes in El Paso, outshining the city's cathedral in annual confirmations and by practically every other measure. It is no surprise, given Calvin's initial unhappiness in Clovis, that he would seek the job. His was an impressive pitch, but it failed.

Various interests and causes occupied Calvin from the beginning of his ministry in Clovis. He headed the local United China Relief Drive, writing and speaking on its behalf. As active in community affairs as his pastoral and teaching duties would permit, Calvin also served on the local United Service Organization at Cannon Army Air Base (now Cannon Air Force Base) west of town and worked to establish a public library for the city. He resurrected "The Parson" column, based upon the model he had successfully launched in Silver City. Unlike there, it was published only weekly and lacked the verve of his Silver City output. Perhaps because of World War II and its attendant calls to faith, many of the columns were centered on religion. One at the end of his second year was entitled "Religion: The World's North Star" (January 31, 1943). Others from the same period were in a similar vein: "Unofficial Pronouncement on Public Morals" (April 13, 1942), "The Church beside the Ice House" (May 10, 1942), "Others Who Are Walking the Same Road" (August 1942). These columns resonated with his strongly faith-based Clovis readership.

Even an article ostensibly about his botanical interests in a January 1943 column in *Southwest Churchman* segued, appropriately enough, considering its venue, into a discussion of plant life in the Holy Land and how it might relate to religious teaching. In referring to a common plant that grows in the Middle East, swaying easily in the wind, Calvin said Jesus did not want such swaying reeds but rather sturdy pillars like John the Baptist upon which to build his church. He likened the prophet to an acacia bush, a plant whose rigid, thorny branches and thin foliage resemble the mesquite of the Southwestern United States. Calvin left behind only a handful of his sermons in his papers, but this could easily have been the framework for one.

St. James achieved the status of a parish, its new designation covered by *Southwest Churchman* in February 1944 in an article titled "A Spectacular Achievement." Calvin threw himself into building a new sanctuary for his flock. The project was destined for success because of Calvin's aggressive fund raising and because he secured John Gaw Meem as its architect. Not long after Calvin arrived at St. James, the parish bought a $100 war bond to kick off the building fund. Getting Meem aboard was the next step. Meem, based in Santa Fe, was a well-regarded architect in New Mexico, best known for helping to pioneer the Pueblo Revival Style. Regarded as one of the most important and influential architects to have worked in the state, Meem designed other churches around the state as well as Zimmerman Library at the University of New Mexico, a campus landmark since 1938 and now the repository for the Calvin Papers. St. James was fortunate to acquire his services. Meem had lifelong ties to the Episcopal Church: His parents had been Episcopal missionaries in Brazil, where he was born. In addition, he served on important diocesan committees. Those considerations may have inclined him toward accepting the St. James's commission because Clovis was then something of a cultural outlier, not known for its architectural renaissance.

Despite Meem's stature, Calvin had his initial doubts about some aspects of the design. He was uncertain whether the new church's appearance would fit in with its surroundings. The church's mission-style construction, so familiar and accepted in Santa Fe, might be considered inappropriate in Clovis. Moreover, as Calvin wrote in *New Mexico Magazine* in an article on the church construction, "a few disapprove, without openly saying so, because the structure has a somewhat Roman Catholic appearance." He feared that could offend the Protestant sensibilities of its neighbors.

Calvin defended selection of the building materials, particularly adobe. That too was not common to the plains. "We didn't select it merely to be archaic and quaint," he explained, but because it is the most appropriate material available in terms of cost and for its natural insulation qualities. Adobe is "an eminently suitable material for a region of wide extremes." It was the same argument for *vigas* (hand-hewn roof beams). If all this were the case, he further argued, the architectural style could be defended as well. Calvin added that "one who knows Southwestern climate is readily persuaded that if the Pueblos and Roman Catholics hadn't devised the low, cube-like style the Baptists would have." Finally, he added that Meem had achieved "high eminence in this style and in this medium." Paradoxically, it is high eminence coupled with simplicity.

St. James is authentic. The forty-pound adobe bricks were made on site. The *vigas* were imported from Santa Fe and then roughhewn with a hand adze. "Native" (Hispanic) labor was used. A Native American master craftsman supervised that phase of the work. The striving for authenticity went so far as to use wooden pegs in lieu of nails. Likewise, the church has no stained glass windows and no murals. Calvin concluded the *New Mexico Magazine* article by observing that "we have ambitiously desired at no time to impress the passing beholder, or to create a big, extended space-covering edifice. Instead we have concentrated a great effort upon something small and precious having...a gemlike perfection." Calvin always considered building the church one of his greatest achievements; as well he should, calling it "one of God's lovely houses." St. James was built "for the exaltation of religion and the delight of those who love beauty."

Building St. James Episcopal Church in Clovis, New Mexico, was one of Calvin's proudest achievements. A post card was made for visitors. (Ross Calvin Papers, Center for Southwest Research, University Libraries, University of New Mexico)

The U.S. State Department disseminated the *New Mexico Magazine* article worldwide to promote good will. Calvin donated his $15 fee to the building fund. The building was essentially paid for upon its completion as Calvin announced in the church bulletin of April 16, 1950.

Calvin's efforts did not go unrecognized by Bishop James M. Stoney, who had succeeded Bartlett. As the bishop noted in his memoir, *Lighting the Candle* (1961), Calvin's work resulted in a new parish body in a little more than two years and, finally, in an edifice "of such exquisite proportions" that it is known as one of "the most beautiful small churches" in the country. In 1943, Bishop Stoney acclaimed St. James "the miracle parish" and continued to do so as he spoke around New Mexico for the next several years. He devoted his entire speech at the fiftieth annual diocesan convention to it.

Rodney Calvin poses in cap and gown following graduation from Clovis, New Mexico High School in 1942. (Ross Calvin Papers, Center for Southwest Research, University Libraries, University of New Mexico)

Although Calvin never taught at Eastern New Mexico College, as he thought he might, he was active there since his responsibilities included looking after its students. Early in World War II, he spoke at a conference on the "Guidance of Youth in a World at War." His topic was "Religion and Patriotism Are Not Electives." Perhaps Calvin was thinking of his son

Rodney, who had joined the Army Air Corps as a nose gunner in 1943 at age nineteen, after graduating from Clovis High School and spending a year at the University of New Mexico. Rodney fought with a squadron based in Guam and charged with harassing Japanese merchant shipping by nighttime strafing and bombing, tearing "their targets to pieces in short order," wreaking carnage on ships and crew alike. On December 22, 1945, Calvin announced in his "Parson" column that he had just received an early Christmas present. Rodney had called just the night before that he was back in the United States and that he was "feeling fine. No tropical diseases, nothing." Calvin wrote that he "knew everything was as usual" when his son asked for money so he could be home for Christmas. Parson titled the column "My Very Special Christmas Present." While Rodney was at war, he had written a "Remember Letter" to his father about the times the two had shared while he was growing up.

Rodney Calvin is shown in flight gear before his barracks. (IHSF.org)

Meanwhile, the Calvins' daughter Peggy was a popular student in Clovis High School and continued to be so when she enrolled at the University of New Mexico. She and her future husband, Edward V. Balcolm, met at Freshman Orientation. He recounted a memory of their first encounter. "She was from the windy east side of the state, and when she tried to lean into the wind in Albuquerque there wasn't any."

U.S. Army Air Corps nose gunner Rodney Calvin was home on leave in Clovis with his sister Peggy and mother Grace. (IHSF.org)

Clovis New Mexico High School student Peggy Calvin. (Ross Calvin Papers, Center for Southwest Research, University Libraries, University of New Mexico)

With Rodney at war and Peggy a busy and popular teen-ager, Calvin and Grace, as much as she was able, had more time to pursue friendships within the church community, bonding more with its members, young and old. Calvin was strongly involved with the children's role in the church. In recalling what it like growing up in the St. James Parish, Martha Choquette recalls Calvin as "the most marvelous man who walked the earth." Calvin baptized her and took an interest in her studies. Martha was thrilled when

Calvin appointed her Sunday school attendance monitor. She remembers, "He was always up at the house visiting with her family," sharing a glass of wine with her parents. When Martha graduated from high school, Calvin gave her an autographed copy of *River of the Sun*, saying it was "one of the very last copies." He expressed hope she would like "the book for itself" and not because it was becoming scarce.

And what had happened meanwhile to Ross Jr.? In 1935 he had graduated from Chrisman Township High School, the same institution his father had attended some thirty years earlier. Always good with his hands, the young man soon found work as an apprentice machinist at the Caterpillar factory in Peoria, Illinois. He rapidly rose to be a tool and die maker. During World War II, he worked on military aircraft engines at the Studebaker Corporation. He joined the Navy toward the end of the war and was stationed first in Chicago. There he met his future wife, Dorothy Ruth Leonhardt, at a USO function. After boot camp, he was transferred to Treasure Island, California, and then to Carmel, California, for radar training. Following the war, like so many World War II veterans, Ross Jr. found he had to reinvent himself.

Intellectually endowed from both parents, but more technically inclined than his mother and father, the young veteran found himself back home in Illinois. Using the GI Bill, he enrolled in Northwestern University, where he earned a B. S. in engineering. Then happenstance came along. A friend and fellow machinist from pre-Navy days called one day to invite Ross Jr. to come to Los Alamos, New Mexico, to look into a possible employment opportunity as a mechanical engineer with the Los Alamos Scientific Laboratory (now known by its acronym LANL because "national" is part of the name). Meetings between Calvin and Ross Jr. were infrequent and brief in those post-World War II days. Charles recalls stopping with his father in the spring or early summer of 1951 in Clovis en route to California when his father was shuttling a car to the West Coast on a paid assignment because the automobile industry could not keep up with new car deliveries in the regular fashion. Charles remembers little save standing in the hot Clovis sun while his grandfather inspected the cream-colored 1950 Ford, nothing of the interactions between the two men. A family visit to Clovis a couple of years later did not go so well, and Charles remembers his father packing up the family and leaving for Los Alamos earlier than planned because of a dispute. Charles also recalls an experience from this visit when his grandfather had him don altar boy garb and "go around lighting and snuffing out candles before and after the ceremony." This was "foreign" to the youngster as he had never before been in an Episcopal church.

The Rev. Ross Calvin and grandson Charles Calvin as an altar boy. (Calvin Family)

Although the younger Calvin's work at LANL was as an engineer, he continued to draw satisfaction from his ability to create devices with his mechanical skills. That sometimes led to his father's misunderstanding and condemnation of his efforts. Ross Jr. had a proclivity for working with his hands because he valued doing so and because his grandparents had provided a model for him. His father, conversely, was a person of ideas and words. The stark contrast in world views and personalities provided "a real anomaly," in the words of Ross Jr.'s son Charles.

When Ross Jr. moved to Los Alamos, the town was still remote because of setting and purpose enveloping its secrecy while the atomic bomb was being developed. Driving time to Santa Fe, the only nearby town of any size, was much longer than today's forty-five minutes. Los Alamos had few retail shops, and they often ran out of supplies. One staple for its drivers was antifreeze to guard against engine damage from the harsh Jemez Mountain winters. Consequently, Ross Jr. would sometimes drive to Santa Fe, cram his station wagon with as much antifreeze as he could buy at $2 a gallon wholesale and then sell it to friends back home for $3. No one objected to the markup because the service station in town charged $6—if it had any at all. Providing automobile supplies went hand-in-hand with Ross Jr.'s pleasure at working on his and neighbors' cars in his backyard shop. Nonetheless, the situation provided another opportunity for his father to vent his displeasure about his firstborn's merchant-like behavior.

10

River of the Sun: The Gila

River of the Sun: Stories of the Storied Gila—Calvin's second major book—met with immediate critical success, nearly equal to that of *Sky Determines*. That one had the Macmillan publicity machine behind it. This one had only the promotion efforts of a regional university press. The book resonated with critics and readers alike as it spoke of a "muddy, deep, and reedy mysterious" *storied* river. *River of the Sun* was accessible; it was also entertaining and educational. In a far-ranging menu of topics beginning with the river's discovery by the Spaniards through the bloody wars with the Apache, Calvin told the Gila's history in tracing its impact upon New Mexico and Arizona for four hundred years. He wrote of people not that long gone and occasionally bridged past and present with interviews of people still alive. He was practicing a form of oral history before it became a commonly accepted practice. Parts of the book read like an adventure novel, except that it is factual, not fiction.

The book is divided into ten chapters, each an independent story or sketch so the reader can dip into it nearly anywhere. Four tell the stories of individuals: Coronado, Kit Carson, Geronimo, and cattleman Tom Lyons. The opening and closing chapter deal with the river itself, and the remainder are about the desert and the river and the efforts to tame them. Each chapter is about fifteen pages in length.

Calvin could take on a preachy tone (appropriately enough, given his primary vocation) as he did when calling the Gila the river of the Apache, who were enabled by right to fight for it—even if the ongoing battles sometimes resulted in a "Roman holiday of blood." The settlers with European roots might call the Apache perpetual war-mongering savages unable to forget the difference between peace and war. Calvin saw it differently: "They lived by [the Gila's] waters in aboriginal times, and they are still here." His implication was that this is their just due.

As much as Calvin admired the Apaches, he also held high regard for the Mormons. His esteem shines through in passages describing their attempts to use the river to irrigate the desert. Sometimes the efforts had unwanted results. In addition to the farmers' constant battle to bring water to the Gila Valley, they also had to guard against those creatures seeking to share the resultant bounty: "Wherever their industry created a succulent, green oasis, there the famished creatures of the desert kept a nocturnal rendezvous." The Mormons also worked with other faiths on other enterprises when needed. The result was that "intelligence brought its own rewards."

Where things had gone wrong, he affixed blame where he thought it belonged. He observed that erosion and its causes had provoked "many short-sighted conservationists" to picture ranchers as the "greediest, most unprogressive lot...in American history." Not so, he countered; many times that was, in fact, far from the truth. He had another culprit in mind. Calvin viewed administration of the public domain upon which many ranchers graze their cattle as a "national stupidity," an opinion he had first articulated two decades earlier. In his "Use/Misuse" article for the Soil Conservation Service, he had termed such actions "the *unwisdom* of the nation." He wrote then that the country was beginning to understand that erosion and flooding were not acts of God, but largely "results of men's folly."

The story of how the book was crafted is fascinating. We are fortunate that Calvin provided a record of the process. In a "Parson" column July 15, 1946, for the *Clovis News-Journal* on "How a Book Is Born," Calvin described researching, writing, fact-checking, and all the mechanical steps involved in its design and production. He offered his own standards for rendering judgment on the book's value: "If the book is remembered by name, read and respectfully consulted ten years after publication—well, you've written something that is altogether exceptional."

The cover of the 1946 University of New Mexico Press edition of *River of the Sun*. (University of New Mexico Press)

When *River of the Sun* was ready for publication, Calvin was a recognized figure in Southwestern literature. He did not have to go hat in hand seeking a publisher. Unlike Macmillan, the University of New Mexico Press was more than willing to publish his new book without asking for a buy-in. Perhaps even more important, the press chose honored book designer Carl Hertzog for the all-important task of crafting the book's physical appearance. Calvin was delighted. He wrote an admirer in early 1946 that as an example of bookmaking the book was "a honey"; design, paper, and typography came together to make *River of the Sun* "something pretty choice." Calvin added that he hoped the contents "don't prove unworthy of the package." Hertzog, who saw book design as a form of the fine arts, set out to print books "of his choice in the style of his choice." This he did with *River of the Sun*. With Hertzog involved, both the printing profession and reviewers greeted its physical appearance with enthusiasm.

Virginia Kirkus, founder of the influential *Kirkus Review*, praised the efforts of both men. She wrote that the book's scholarly approach surpassed previous attempts on the subject. It was, she observed, "more sober, more scientific" with greater human interest. At the same time, *River of the Sun* was "one of the finest pieces of bookmaking of the year." *Chicago Tribune* called it an "exquisitely printed book" and "one of the handsomest of the year." *Forth*, a lesser-known journal, called it "beautiful to handle, charming to read, authentic as to fact." The printing profession was likewise complimentary. The American Institute of Graphic Arts designated it as a monthly selection for "typographic design and excellence." Willard Hougland, editor of *Southwest Review*, said Calvin's new book "can well take its place along...*Sky Determines*" and complimented the University of New Mexico Press for its "fine production." Several reviewers thought it worthwhile to mention the inclusion of ten black and white photographs, three provided by Calvin.

John Weld commented in *The New York Times*, "Truly the Gila deserved a chronicler and truly the Rev. Ross Calvin was the man to write it." Weld wrote that Calvin believed the Gila to be the "most beautiful spot on Earth" and "he rises to rhapsodic heights" to say so. *Arizona Monthly* devoted eight pages with a reproduction of the book's cover and half a dozen photos by both Calvins and renowned photographer Joseph Muench. Its attempt at critical commentary was to quote an unidentified source: "to limn the turbulent steam from its fount to its juncture...and from the time when the memory of man runneth not to the contrary to this day." The book ranked as high as number two in the *New York Herald Tribune Weekly Book Review*.

Unlike the denser, more thought-provoking *Sky Determines*, *River of the Sun* is for the most part easy and pleasant reading, yet informative to even an unschooled readership. That was Erna Fergusson's view when, in her review for *New York Herald Tribune Weekly Book Review*, she called it "altogether... an authentic book, valuable as an introduction to a region of strange beauty." Calvin's prose was as beautiful as the country he was writing about. His words could sing; they could be eloquent—he wrote with "the fervor of a poet." She went on, "The Gila is little known though its legends are legion," but *River of the Sun* is packed with Calvin's "close observations" delivered with "the kindness of a friend." Thinking of *Sky Determines*, she told her readers that Calvin "has done it again." To her the Gila was an important river not only in the history of its own watershed but of the United States as well.

Joseph Henry Jackson reminded readers of his widely read *San Francisco Chronicle* "Bookman's Notebook" that "white men saw the Southwest [and the Gila]...long before Plymouth or Jamestown." He wrote that Calvin was "eminently suited" for the task of writing *River of the Sun* and the book richly deserved its appellation. "More Americans like him [Calvin] should be writing...regional books," he declared. If this were the case, "more would come out of regionalism." Jackson held that Calvin's prose "is first rate" and his observations "shrewd," allowing him to approach his topic in a "pleasant leisurely fashion" while employing a "quiet gentle reflectiveness." He saw Calvin as "a curious blend of poet, scientist, historian and essayist," making the combination "ideal for the job he...sets out to do." Calvin's kind of writing gives the reader "all the liveliness he could ask," for Calvin always "balances his book excellently."

With his new book, it was inevitable there would be comparisons with the first one. Thus Calvin must have been pleased at Stanley Vestal's words in *The Saturday Review of Literature*: "Ross Calvin does not turn out a book nearly as often" as his readers would like, so when a new book of his appears, it is "worth waiting for." He pointed out how Calvin displayed his subjects by topics, with "each chapter having its own chronology, background, and incident." *The Christian Century* agreed with Vestal's estimation of the book's worth. While *Sky Determines* was "one of the best books ever written" about New Mexico, it held *River of the Sun* was of "the same quality." The book was "a scholarly and readable account" of "an old and storied land."

Back home, the *Clovis News-Journal* called it "another great book" on the Southwest, particularly of the Gila River country, "a scholarly book." *New Mexico Magazine* in its lukewarm three-inch mention allowed that it a "very readable" book and a "really fine" contribution to the Southwestern canon. *El Palacio*, the Museum of New Mexico's journal, by contrast, offered a more complete, sympathetic view. It printed a full synopsis, observing that Calvin had "painted a vivid and sympathetic picture" of life along the Gila. Calvin's prose, the reviewer wrote, "moves with the flow" of the river.

University of Arizona historian Frank C. Lockwood, in writing of the book for the *Arizona Daily Star*, offered another balanced, penetrating view. Like Fergusson, he acknowledged Calvin's ability to convey a "certain magic" when writing of the Southwest. Lockwood wrote that *River of the Sun* combined "a rare degree" of scholarship and literary style and that it was "a delightful work, pleasant to look at, to handle, and to read." He faulted only what he perceived as the book's unevenness in its "proportion and balance." Lockwood believed Calvin devoted too much attention to New Mexico and not enough to Arizona, through which the river makes much of its way to its confluence with the Colorado. It may rise in New Mexico's Mogollons, he conceded, but the Gila is chiefly an Arizona river. Lockwood also saw the book lacking in "organic principle," its "proportion and balance" not that good. Instead of the chapters being "bright marbles in a bag," they would have been better conceived as "a cluster of grapes on its parent vine."

Lockwood also considered the chapter on Tom Lyons, which attracted such controversy from within Lyons's family, to be "extraneous in both spirit and matter." Lockwood thought Lyons "a sensational resident of Silver City" but "insignificant as an individual." Someone said Calvin's problem with the Lyons clan was that he had provided "an unvarnished account" of the man. Lyons might have been colorful, but he did not do enough in developing the cattle industry and the Southwest to merit the attention he received. Lockwood suggested other subjects more worthy of inclusion, most of them from Arizona. Lockwood tempered his criticism by acknowledging that Calvin was "an original thinker" about the Southwest and that he knew of "no other book that contains so much in so little" and was so delightfully written.

The Tom Lyons sketch, in fact, brought cries of outrage from his family as "a cruelly false and distorted account." Lyons's family would have agreed with Lockwood that the chapter should have been omitted, but because they thought it defamed their kinsman. "It was with horror and amazement that I read your outrageous chapter," read one charge. Calvin's depiction of Lyons was a perpetuation of "a cruelly false and distorted account," said another. "A vicious article of truths [perverted into] half-truths, insinuations, and prevarications," said still another. These observations are illustrative of the outrage voiced much later by Lyons relatives Ida Foster Campbell and Alice Foster Hill in their *Triumph and Tragedy: A History of Thomas Lyons and the LCs* (2003).

River of the Sun engendered misstatements and misunderstandings from still other sources. A history of the Church of the Good Shepherd notes that Calvin published *River of the Sun* to pay for a furnace for the rectory to keep his family warm. The book came out in 1946; the Calvins had departed Silver City in January 1942. Many years later, Calvin recorded having installed a gas furnace in the rectory on November 4, 1936, with the notation that "we paid for it!" The church history also alleges that a parishioner had obtained an injunction to stop Calvin from selling any copies. There is no record of such. Perhaps the church historian was thinking of the time an attorney for the Lyons family advised them to avoid doing anything that would make the book more widely read.

Calvin had soldiered on, and his perseverance made it worthwhile. In writing of the Gila, he became its tutelary. The inspiration the book engenders bears that out. The Gila is a treasured source of live-giving water for Arizona and New Mexico. Its history, beauty, and mystery attract people of all backgrounds—artists, hikers, outdoorsman, and those seeking solitude and quietude. Today, as New Mexico's last wild river, the Gila is a magnet for those who would tame it for their use but equally a source of passion for those who would leave it as it is. It has an important place in the region's collective psyche.

Bill Toth, professor of English at Western New Mexico University, who writes on Southwestern literature, believes the Gila still has not received the literary acclaim it is due. "Other Southwestern rivers have their literary champions," he notes. "The Gila...has precious few." Many authorities believe the Gila to be "the quintessential" Southwestern river, he observes. With its own ecosystem, the Gila is "unique" in its ecology: "There's really nothing else quite like it in all of the American Southwest... [and] yet so few have written about it competently." Among Toth's "few" are Edwin Corle, author of *The Gila: River of the Southwest* (1965), and M. H. "Dutch" Salmon, long a defender of the Gila, who has written *¡Gila Libre!* (2008) and *Gila Descending* (2009). Toth calls Corle's *Gila* "a fine book," but believes *River of the Sun* is "the better" of the two. He further argues that *River of the Sun* and *Sky Determines* are two of the "most critically important investigations" of Southwestern ecology and human history ever written. "Nothing surpasses them." In Toth's view, Calvin has "long deserved" more critical attention than he has received.

The Books of the Colorado River and the Grand Canyon: A Selective Bibliography (1953) praised *River of the Sun* for its "unusual insight" into the character of the region. In 1958, *Arizona Highways* included it in *A Southwestern Century: One Hundred Definitive Books Which Best Tell the Story of the Southwest*, compiled by Calvin's champion Lawrence Clark Powell. Thomas C. Donnelly, later the tenth president of New Mexico Highlands University after leaving University of New Mexico, predicted that *River of the Sun* "will live a long time."

11

Later Publications

The immediate post-World War II years in Clovis were busy, productive ones for Calvin. He was turning out more writing in addition to his church duties. Besides *River of the Sun* in 1946 and the second edition of *Sky Determines* in 1948, he wrote an important scholarly paper in 1947. It was sociological in orientation as he examined those New Mexicans who peopled the east and west sides of the state. "The People of New Mexico" gave Calvin another chance to prove he was more than just a student and chronicler of the natural world. He could study and report on his fellow humans in their environment as well. The Division of Research, Department of Government, at the University of New Mexico gave him the chance.

In his letter requesting the paper, the director, Thomas C. Donnelly, confessed that "it's this simple: the kind of government and politics we have in New Mexico is very much a product of the kind of people who live here. People thinking about how to improve things need to know a little more about the raw material they have to work with and so on." Calvin agreed with the offer and the premise, saying his study of the state and its people "began the day I arrived." He saw that "a comparative study" of Silver City and Clovis would provide "a good springboard" of the two sides of the state and their inhabitants. Calvin told

Donnelly he had ministered not only to "fairly comfortable Episcopalians" but to diverse groups as well. He felt "most at home," he confessed, among college students and their instructors, but the friendships "I valued most" were miners, ranchers, and government men.

The resulting thirty-eight page monograph has been called "a significant brochure" more than once by editors and scholars. It was a marked departure from Calvin's mainstream writing though he used the same analytical skills in examining people as he did in nature, falling back on traditional rhetorical principles to highlight things he found alike or different. Calvin wrote of the two areas' politics, life-styles, and mind-sets. His aim, as Donnelly had directed, was to provide a basis for decision making at political, social, and economic levels for individuals, governments, and businesses. He called upon his fifteen years in Silver City in the southwestern corner of the state and the five he had spent so far in Clovis almost midway on the state's eastern border, providing insight into his fellow residents' foibles and follies. A footnote to the essay observes that "having spent his entire New Mexico sojourn in the two towns, he knows them well, loves them both!"

His observations were for the most part spot on and are still pertinent today. Sometimes his biases slip through: he preferred his adopted southwestern section. Between the two areas "there is [in the southwest] an interesting and well-defined difference which begins in topography and extends into the realm of human concerns." The eastern side, he notes, is "far less cosmopolitan" and less "deeply tinged" by what he called the "Spanish" influence. He notes too a matter of age: Clovis, the principal city of the area, was but forty years old. Silver City dated to the 1870s.

Using the term "culture" to embrace occupation, religion, recreation, and intellectual climate, Calvin wrote that "one may see instantly" that the culture of Silver City is purely Western and Clovis Midwestern. Silver City's streets and saloons, once bustling with army officers from nearby Fort Bayard and mining men, were never seen in Clovis. (There were servicemen of course during Calvin's tenure in Clovis during World War II.) The Fort Bayard soldiers had served everywhere and "carried with them their own cosmopolitan ideas of a good time." The mining men, many of whom had plied their profession in South America, were "a hearty outdoor breed who without apology liked their whisky straight and plentiful." Calvin did not neglect to mention the ranchers whose cowboys "set a high standard of roistering" once they got to town. Health seekers, furthermore, were drawn to Silver City because of the restorative powers of its clean, sparkling air, and that in turn "created a tradition of sophisticated gaiety." One can almost read the pity in Calvin's voice for the poor deprived east siders who had to find their solace inside church walls. As he once observed, the Great Plains upon which Clovis sits, produces a kind of "emotional starvation."

It was on the matter of religion that, as a churchman, Calvin drew his sharpest distinctions. Here he found the religious climate of Silver City "less satisfactory" as contrasted with an abundance of churches and churchgoers in Clovis, which he characterized as the hub of the Bible Belt. Here, the contrast between Clovis and Silver City "emerges most clearly." He begins by noting that in Silver City there was "a gratifying absence of censoriousness and hypocrisy." In contrast, "Clovis proudly and defiantly claims to be part of the Bible-belt. Their mores prevail. They set the standards—standards oftentimes illiberal." He offers a particularly biting observation: "Hypocrisy flourishes in Clovis because it is good policy to appear religious. In Silver City hypocrisy hardly exists. There is so little need for it." Remarkably, those comments did not boomerang back on him. In fact, if there was any substantial reaction to his paper, positive or negative, from citizens of either town, I have not found it. The paper earned him $100.

His next major undertaking was the introduction and the notes for the University of New Mexico's 1951 reprint of *Lieutenant Emory Reports: A Reprint of Lieutenant W. H. Emory's Notes of a Military Reconnoissance* [sic] originally published by order of Congress in 1848. The University of New Mexico Press director, E. B. Mann, must have thought Calvin a natural fit for the assignment because of Calvin's ever-increasing reputation as a scholar and a naturalist. Indeed, it would have been difficult to find anyone to match his unique set of skills. It was a fortuitous association for both parties. After *Sky Determines* and *River of the Sun*, *Lieutenant Emory Reports* is Calvin's most referenced publication. Calvin called the book "a gold mine of accurate, first-hand observations" characterized by "a three-dimensional vividness." He praised Emory's botanical abilities, remarking that his contributions to the scientific knowledge of the Southwest were "highly valued." Calvin noted with particular enthusiasm Emory's prodigious discoveries of many new species.

Ever the stickler for correct scientific nomenclature, he found relatively little with which to fault Emory. He noted misspellings of some place-names and in the naming of some indigenous peoples Emory had encountered. Calvin reserved his most severe criticism for the incorrect naming of a spring, which should have been called the San Vicente, around which later sprang the village which became Silver City. In the overall scope of things though, these are very minor flaws in Emory's chronicling a laborious, sometimes dangerous, military excursion into what is now the American Southwest that began in the summer of 1846 in Fort Leavenworth and ended in San Diego, California, in January 1847.

Ironically, although Emory discovered a new species of oak later named *Quercus emoryi*, he took but little notice of crossing the highest point of New Mexico's Black Range, which today bears his name. For that honor, Calvin claims credit. On October 17, 1846, Emory noted the summit "was so indistinct [it is 8227 feet above sea level] that I passed it [by] several miles before discovering it." A present-day marker notes that Emory "may have crossed at another pass south of here." Calvin was more certain of his facts. In a July 12, 1938, "Village Parson" column in the *Silver City Daily Press* he had asked, "What do you call the highest point between Silver City and the Rio Grande?" In a subsequent column three days later, headlined "Emory Pass is Now Named," he provided the answer. Since there was no official designation either on the marker or on the map, Calvin jumped in. "We have named it, to be sure," he exclaimed. Emory Pass it became; Emory Pass it remains.

The University of New Mexico Press edition of *Lieutenant Emory Reports* met with limited, but favorable, critical reception. Surely the most pleasing to Calvin must have been a review in *The New York Times* from University of Texas English professor and acclaimed Western chronicler J. Frank Dobie. Dobie lamented the omission of engravings of flora Emory's party had encountered but graciously noted that "cherishers" of the original "may feel compensated" by Calvin's interpretative notes. The *El Paso Herald-*

Post continued in a similar vein by observing that the "scholarly rector" had added "another distinguished volume to his list." Other newspapers resonated with similar praise.

In his introduction to the *Lieutenant Emory Reports*, Calvin credits Emory for being one of his forerunners who led him to botany. He had already devoted considerable attention to another mentor in "Some Southwestern Naturalists" (*New Mexico Quarterly Review*, 1949). In the Reverend Edward Lee Greene, Calvin found a role model in both the scientific and vocational senses, for Greene, like Calvin, had been a rector at the Church of the Good Shepherd. Greene was the epitome of the peripatetic parson even in an age when long-distance walking was common. As Calvin relates it, Greene arrived on foot in Silver City in 1876, not long after the village's founding, without church credentials to minister to a tiny new flock in the young rough-and-ready mining town. Remarkably, he had walked the entire way from San Diego, California, a distance of more than six hundred miles through mostly desert. Greene may have received a call from above for his new posting, but it was clear what motivated him—the chance to observe and collect botanical specimens along the way. Calvin admired Greene in that he "had no hesitation" in saying "he found botany more fascinating" than theology. "To him," Calvin wrote, "belongs the honor of introducing to science 171 new species."

John C. Van Dyke was another exemplar of a traveler with a keen eye for nature and the stories it revealed as he trudged alone during some three years, save for an Indian pony and his fox terrier, Cappy. Van Dyke crisscrossed the deserts of California, Arizona, and parts of Mexico in the late 1800s. Like Calvin, he too was a health seeker, an educated man from the East who found more than a restored body in the solitude and grandeur of the West. Calvin credited Van Dyke directly for inspiring him "in so many ways." He had particular praise for the "surprising accuracy" Van Dyke, an art critic from Princeton and Harvard, displayed in his observations of plants and animals, "but above all, how sensitive he was to desert light and air." Lawrence Clark Powell quoted Calvin as saying in a 1964 letter that Van Dyke was the most influential source on his writing.

For all his botanical interests, Calvin wrote only one quasi-scholarly article on the subject. This was "The Exotic Plants of New Mexico," which appeared in *Mosaic of New Mexico's Scenery, Rocks, and History* for the New Mexico Bureau of Mines and Mineral Resources in 1964, with reprints in 1967 and 1972. Given Calvin's interest in the close relation between "certain plants and certain rocks and soils," the choice of venue is no surprise. The piece, however, was tailored to fit the book's subtitle: *A Brief Guide for Visitors*. Rather than being "exotic," his choices were frequently found plants in New Mexico, familiar to natives, who encountered them everywhere even if they did not know their Latin names. Although Calvin said discussing the state's plant life "might be complicated" for some, he set forth his observations clearly and concisely.

Calvin kept a list of his major published material, including books and articles, numbering at least 115. He once expressed a hope to the *El Paso Herald-Post* that his columns might be syndicated. It did not happen. His writing for religious publications was scant, and what does exist may not be on strictly religious subjects. For example, in 1948 *Southern Churchman* published his "Testimony of Music." (A year earlier Calvin had published an article in *The Etude* titled "Late Blooming Organist.") Somehow he now found time to write ten full-length articles for *New Mexico Magazine*, nearly matching what he had produced for it earlier. Tom Hester has singled out one of those, "Tularosa Basin Is a Museum," as representative of Calvin's forward thinking. Hester says the March 1949 article anticipates the idea of regional museums, an idea that became particularly popular during the 1970s. Regional museums concern themselves with the culture, history, environment, social development, and language of their region. Calvin wrote that if one could select one spot in New Mexico and then write about it, photograph it, and study it, the effort would focus attention upon man's environment and its effect upon his ways. Calvin's idea was to select a significant location and make "the place, not a big building" into a regional museum. The Tularosa Basin satisfied his criteria. For him, it was "an introduction to the desert."

He tried to get paid when he could. In the late 1940s he wrote two essays for Western Scenic Views *See Your West Series*, sponsored by the Standard Oil Company. There were multiple authors for the series (Dobie was one) and lots of photographs. They were apparently available as spiral-bound booklets at gas stations. Calvin earned $200 for each piece. Joseph Henry Jackson had suggested him for the assignment. The first to appear was on Shiprock. The acclaimed Ansel Adams provided photographs for the second on White Sands National Monument.

Several of his *New Mexico Magazine* articles were puff pieces intended to promote tourism. One historical piece provided the story of the Church of the Apostles in Las Trampas, New Mexico. Four more replicated the flavor of his early Log Books. They were called "A Naturalist's Notebook," reflecting observations back to 1942 and beginning with the somewhat self-deprecatory "since the *mature* [italics added] age of twelve I have kept a naturalist's log book." His account dealt with "things that grow, things that run, things that fly." He followed that a month later, further explaining his purpose and method: "My Log Book, while chronological, is not a diary but a record of field trips—though sometimes... [they] were made by train, sometimes by boat, sometimes in car or on horseback. The best of all were made on foot." He recalled how the trips began in Illinois and included a sojourn in New England and residence in Pennsylvania and New York. In covering many parts of the country, they also covered many types of terrain. The series concluded in April 1961. In the last article, Calvin nostalgically revisited a young farm boy's initiation into "the mystical brotherhood of naturalists" on a hot summer morning when he inadvertently flushed a great blue heron from a sluggish stream bed on the Illinois prairie. "As it took heavily to the air in surprise...there came over me a breath-stopping excitement and delight that can never be erased from my memory."

As much of a pleasure as it was for Calvin to continuing writing about his abiding love for New Mexico, near the end of his life he returned to his early association with the church in the East to produce a totally different kind of book. *Barnabas in Pittsburgh: From Common Clay to Legend* (1966) was a new kind of writing challenge, but an equally agreeable one. For the first time, Calvin tried his hand at an extended biography. The book was a labor of love: "an act of devotion," in his words. It was just as well because the book attracted little public attention when it was issued by the Carlton Press, a New York City vanity press. The book is a testimony to and celebration of the life of Gouverneur Provoost Hance, SBB, the founder of the St. Barnabas Brotherhood and Free Home in Pittsburgh for incurably ill boys and men when there was no insurance or governmental coverage. He operated it from its opening in 1900 until his death in 1954.

Calvin likely saw the book as a tribute to his second wife since Hance was her uncle. The family frequently vacationed there from Silver City, and Calvin wrote of it in his newspaper columns. Calvin tried to explain to his newspaper readers back home how the couple could find peace in this shelter for the unfortunate in an environment as unlike their Southwestern home as could be. He anticipated such skepticism: "Now I hear you say under your breath, 'What a place to spend a vacation!'" Another time he noted that at St. Barnabas "everything falls in the simple routine of labor and prayer." As Calvin observed, "It was never contemplated that prayer and work…should be two separate compartments. They interpenetrate and suffuse each other absolutely."

In an undated, unpublished, essay about the book entitled "That Gold Chasuble," Calvin remarked that *Barnabas* was an "unexcited narrative" of someone who "never felt himself 'sainted,' never imagined himself storming up to the gate of heaven." The St. Barnabas journal, *Faith and Work*, called Calvin's book "as reasonably accurate" as possible in tracing Hance's founding of the home. Unfortunately, the book is effusive and overwritten. Inspired it may be; inspiring it is not. Now seventy-seven years old, Calvin was ending his writing career on a muted note.

12

Family Matters

Consecration of the new church in Clovis on September 12, 1950, marked completion of a major task. Calvin had little more to accomplish there. The end of his active ministry was drawing nigh. He enjoyed the new St. James church seven years before retirement December 31, 1957. He had just turned sixty-eight, and all he had known was study and work. It was time for a new life in Albuquerque with time for travel, leisure, study, and reflection. But he was plagued with terrible, dark thoughts.

His family, parishioners, and friends would have been horrified had they known of a deeply personal three-paragraph reflection called "Thoughts in front of a crucifix on a 68th birthday" that he wrote a month before retirement. Its image was so strong and the message so powerful that L. G. Moses chose it to begin his essay on Calvin. It revealed that in Calvin's deepest, innermost thoughts all was darkness; everything was spiraling downward, out-of-control. The first line sets the tone: "I have never believed this life is worth living." The rest is no brighter: "Unless there be something beyond it infinitely better, I should think it a more fortunate fate not to be born."

When Calvin expressed the fear that Grace seemed to be lapsing into "incurable madness," he asked what "hath she done to deserve this fate?" From there, it was a quick progression to "the horror" overshadowing their children and grandchildren. "Guiltless they stand, like their mother, within the shadow" of its ramifications. Calvin wondered if he had "inflicted" this "fate" on them. He continued, "I watch this horror encroaching day by day, and I live in hell, helpless." He then referred to the chasm between him and Ross Jr.: "If from this nightmare there could be in the morning a merciful awakening! But the tomorrow will be as today."

All this was in stark contrast to his public pronouncements. He had told parishioners some two years earlier the time to retire is "while the sun is fairly high in the west, not at sunset." It was not mandatory retirement, he reminded them. Nor had it been brought on by the "imminent onset of extreme old age" or "serious health issues." It was just time. In fact, he noted, "I can still walk erect [and, referring to a summer's softball game,] I can still hit a pitched ball and still run the bases." Calvin simply wanted to enjoy "the harvest years" to continue his lifelong pursuit of learning. He set the scene for his departure at Christmas services, noting that "this holy season marks the parting of the ways. When it ends I shall be entering upon an uncharted life of leisure and study." He concluded his farewell sermon by harkening back to "this noble, and now famous church building. We rejoiced together on the day it was completed, paid for, consecrated forever, to the worship of Almighty God. I have loved it since the massive walls first began to rise. I love it now and shall always love it."

Grace's steady decline became a long and continuing source of disquiet. Calvin became concerned that her illness might have been passed on to her children. His granddaughter Dr. Teresa Balcomb several years later told her cousin Mary Calvin that Grace had a form of Chorea (involuntary arm movements or flinging), but definitely not Parkinson's Disease or Huntington's Chorea. (That "flinging" could explain what Rodney observed in Grace's Silver City kitchen so many years before.) The episode was disquieting for everyone. "She just wasn't functional the last few years," says her grandson John Randall. The signs became more persistent and more troubling. In April 1957, Calvin wrote old Clovis friends Charlie and Marty Mauldin from St. Barnabas House, where the couple was resting: "Grace is not well. Far from it. Am greatly worried." Her condition was not to get better.

On March 30, 1960, State District Judge Robert W. Reidy committed

Grace to the State Hospital in Las Vegas. From there the Medical Administrative Assistant, Albert E. Ball, conveyed a message that put Calvin's mind to rest: Rodney and Peggy could not have inherited her illness. In October of that year, the medical staff examined Grace; Ball assured Calvin that there was "no basis to any kind of concern for your children in this respect." Grace died in the hospital on January 21, 1961. Someone (Calvin or Ball?) wrote at the bottom of the announcement, "Cause of death: 'generalized arteriosclerosis.' (Official)." Grace was buried in Albuquerque's Fairview Memorial Cemetery, where her husband would later be interred. Her gravestone reads "Grace Van D. CALVIN 1899–1961."

With Grace gone, Calvin became more sentient of the gulfs within his family. He sought to span it with letters, face-to-face meetings, and sometimes larger gatherings approaching the status of mini family reunions. There were intermittent attempts at reconciliation with his firstborn, but they often went awry. Calvin's fault-finding took many forms, even faulting Ross Jr.'s simple neighborly actions. During a family get-together he expressed dismay over his son's dealing in "black market" commodities, alluding to the anti-freeze runs to Santa Fe. He decried Ross Jr.'s "blue collar" roots, despite his having a degree from Northwestern. The elder Calvin seemed not to understand why someone who had the possibility of escaping from his background chose not to. As this book nears completion, Ross Jr. is still alive at age ninety-seven. He speaks little of days past, but, armed with a personal computer, he has become a prodigious recorder of memories of his earlier life.

Charles, in pondering why emotional reconciliation became a virtual impossibility, cites a damning postscript to an earlier letter Calvin had written to Ross Jr.: "I would prefer you change your name. [Your] having my name is a reminder of a paternity of which I am not proud." Effects of this letter and its addendum lingered. Ross Jr. would pull it out every time he wanted to dwell on his feelings of mistreatment, says his son: "In many ways, it was a kind of organizing principle of my father's life—his [sense of] abandonment and rejection." Charles acknowledges that his understanding of the Ross-Ross Jr. dynamics "is almost all derived through the lens of my father's perception. I don't think he [Ross Jr.] ever understood why his father's feelings changed toward him."

Calvin did write to his grandchildren, and often. Charles was a frequent recipient of his correspondence, as was granddaughter Teresa. Recalling her birth, Calvin told the girl that grandmother Grace was "still beautiful and well." He wrote that "it is impossible for you to realize that your grandparents haven't always been old—and unattractive." That engendered thoughts of his own grandparents, especially his grandfather, Raleigh Calvin, who did not evoke tender remembrances: "He wasn't very attractive to me in my childhood." His grandfather had made him seem foolish as a boy when he was suddenly asked, "What is arithmetic?" With no answer promptly forthcoming, the older man retorted that arithmetic was the science of art and numbers. "So he always made me a little afraid of him." The pity is that Calvin apparently never saw he was following in his grandfather's footsteps. Luckily, Calvin had found his own father a marked contrast: "My own dear father" never made him fearful, "and I don't remember that he ever laid a hand on me in punishment, for I was always trained not to disobey him."

Even as Calvin showed his doting grandfatherly side in his letter to Teresa, he also exhibited a practical one as well. Telling her that he thought she had "all the toys and dresses you need," he wrote, "I'm going to give you for your birthday another check for your bank account. I have five lovely little granddaughters now and I want to make sure that each one of them has some money as a start for her education." Teresa put her education kitty to good use; at the time of the publication of this book, she is an MD in Albuquerque.

In writing to another granddaughter, he added his continuing stricture about the value of education: "[That] which has always been needful is now more so than ever, for it has become an exacting and costly necessity. In the competition of life today each little girl must be educated, well groomed, and skilled in some of the arts such as music, dancing, swimming, riding, and so on." He also noted the value of religion: "While it might be possible to have manners without religion, it's certainly impossible to have religion without manners." He reminded her that "good manners start from a kind heart." As he had done with Teresa, Calvin enclosed a $10 check for her education fund.

Calvin attempted to ensure that one Calvin beside himself would get into Harvard. Perhaps it could be Charles. He wrote the Harvard admissions office urging it to take another look at the young man's application. (He had been placed on a waiting list.) Calvin suggested that perhaps an Eastern boy already accepted into Harvard would prefer a Western school and thus relieve the pressure "partly enough" to leave "a single vacancy" for his grandson. Calvin said he realized from his own experience that entry into Harvard was "an iron chain that does not stretch." But he pulled out all the stops, including mention of his two degrees from Harvard and Adine's master's from Radcliffe. He ended by saying that he wanted only "the flat-footed truth" about his grandson's chances. Harvard was not persuaded; the boy was not admitted. Charles remembers his grandfather being more disappointed than he was. Meanwhile, he had been admitted to Pomona College in California. He took a BA degree there cum laude. "Still," he adds, when it came time for law school, "I recall a slightly unseemly feeling of satisfaction when I informed Harvard Law School that I'd decided to go to Yale instead." He is now an attorney in Denver.

Calvin's relations with his second son, despite whatever might have passed between them during Rodney's adolescence, improved upon the young man's return from fighting in World War II. Calvin wrote a number of columns about his son during the war, recounting the young man's travails. On one Father's Day, Calvin recounted a letter from Rodney, who was still in a military hospital with pneumonia. He called it "a Remember Letter" in which he recalled episodes in their life. Calvin concluded that "there is no higher ambition in my heart" than to be the kind of father to Rodney his father was to him.

Warm feeling surfaced again between father and son a few years later, following Rodney's marriage, as he and Christine sought advice on naming their first child. Calvin replied that it was well to have "a good Christian name." He suggested his wife's surname of Van Deurs Hance. "Van D. always looks good on a visiting card," he offered. Calvin explained that "an old family name [surname] usually makes a better choice than two given names." When the baby was born May 3, 1953, he became John Randall Calvin.

As the boy matured into adolescence, his grandfather would sometimes share advice. As for financial practices, he would offer: "Remember: You always make your money while you're sleeping." This was an apparent reference to the machinations of Wall Street, two time zones removed from the Mountain

West. Another aphorism was "when you go to a new place always meet your banker first, your lawyer second, and your priest third." His grandson believes that was intended as advice from a man of the world as well as a spiritual one.

As Calvin moved into his twilight years his three children were all still alive, married, and with children of their own. Ross Jr. had five children, Rodney three, and Peggy two. Rodney lived on until 1987. Peggy lived until 2006.

13

Cultivating His Garden

*—Cela est bien dit, répondit Candide,
mais il faut cultiver notre jardin.*

Whether Calvin harkened to *Candide* or not, when he left Clovis to live out his retirement years in Albuquerque, cultivate his garden he did, along with a host of other activities that filled his days the last thirteen years of his life. Like Candide, Calvin finally found some degree of peace at the end of his tribulations after searching for happiness in a sometimes-troubled personal life and in questing for professional achievement and recognition. He was wise enough to rest and be content, determined to value what he had at last attained. In some ways, the roughly last fifth of his life was the most tranquil of all. Only the very end reveals that dark forces still held sway.

Much of Calvin's tranquility can be traced to his garden. He derived a good deal of solace from it and enjoyed thinking aloud about his vision of the ideal garden. Sharing "Confessions of an Illegitimate Gardener" with a garden-club audience in 1965, he did just that while poking a little fun at himself in the process. Falling back on his self-deprecating description of himself as only "something of a botanist," Calvin confided that he had a "modest store of knowledge" of plant ecology. So, as he put it facetiously, he was "Not a real gardener but an irregular botanist." It was just not enough, he confided, to qualify him as "a practical, card-carrying real gardener." It was a light-hearted approach to a delightful and thoughtful topic.

Ross Calvin enjoyed the solace and pleasure of his gardens. (Ross Calvin Papers, Center for Southwest Research, University Libraries, University of New Mexico)

Calvin held, "A garden needs something more than flowers alone." A true garden, he felt, "needs the great four-inch Turnus butterflies, and the humming of bees in the larkspurs and hollyhocks, and the rasping of katydids in late summer evenings to warn that frost is lurking in the long nights ahead." (His choice of words suggests that he may have been thinking of his own approaching end.) More, "a garden needs birds too." Robins and linnets first, then in the warm September afternoons the "illegitimate gardener" welcomes tanagers, warblers, and sparrows to his woodbines "where they devour the purple grapelike berries."

Natural things need artifice also: "There should be a vase or two whose lines will add grace and symmetry to a leafy background." Not content with pottery alone, Calvin believed there should be "a well on which to train English ivy or a creeper." He further thought "a garden gate with a bell to ring a welcome to visitors is almost a must." Old bottles "to imprison sunbeams" would be pleasant, but "above all, a garden needs a sundial—above all else, that is, save memories...." Memories were a subject the speaker did not choose to pursue with his listeners. He had too many as his end days approached, not all of which he wanted to share.

Five years before his death, Calvin spoke further of retirement and time in his garden. He wrote of his small, walled-in garden in Albuquerque and a life "not altogether lonely, with grandchildren...with leisure for study, and for the cultivation of a literary style which aspires...toward the ease and grace" of classic English prose. That was a goal he had quested after all his life and one realized more than he knew. A garden, he wrote, is a "great revealer" of one's philosophy. He also unveiled an aspect of his retirement years that few knew anything of—the study of mathematics, "where I am undoing by a little the most regretted error (intellectual, that is) of my youth," as he told a student. (Was he thinking of his grandfather's question about arithmetic?) Again, as if looking forward to his final years, he employed the metaphor of his sundial, "which recalls for the hours of solitude former seed-times, recurring snows and winter nights, hopes, regrets, partings, time's injustices. So run the years accumulating into slow decades, the fifth, the sixth and so on as the century nears the last third of its annual circuits. October's here already!"

Calvin had given some forty years' professional service to his church. He continued to be actively involved. He was named canon honorary at St. John's Cathedral in Albuquerque upon moving there. In that role he was often called upon to fill in and preach as needed. As one would expect, listeners took away very different versions of both what he said and how he said it. Lacking written copies, we have no basis to judge for ourselves. Linda Shay, now an active member of the Church of the Good Shepherd, remembers occasionally being taken as a girl from church to church in Albuquerque by her parents and finding Calvin's sermons "more like a lecture than a sermon."

Ross Calvin looked forward to reading and study in retirement. Here he pauses in his home in Albuquerque in October of 1962. (Ross Calvin Papers, Center for Southwest Research, University Libraries, University of New Mexico)

Grandson John Randall Calvin, on the other hand, remembers, "His sermons were almost like music. He was so articulate that he could hold an entire congregation in his hand. He was not anything like you would think of as a priest. He was not a Bible thumper; he didn't try to beat his ideas into anyone." John Randall remembers Calvin's sermons more "ad lib, spontaneous, and story-like" than those delivered from a prepared text. He recalls his grandfather's stories, sometimes based on his life, were connected to scripture and the lesson he was trying to impart. In one place he might be passionate like an actor striding across the stage or then with clerical robes flowing as he paced the aisles. In another he would be gesticulating and punching the air to make a point. He used the same oratorical style when he preached in pueblo churches as far west as Acoma and north to Santo Domingo along the Rio Grande and all the way up to Colorado with his grandson in tow.

Once Calvin was out of the church environment he could show a completely different side of himself. He could be stern and "self-absorbed and high minded" as well as "extremely demanding and egocentric," says his grandson. The older man was "not pretentious" but did have "a high opinion of himself." John Randall feels that "he was somehow tortured in many ways that kept him out of touch with his more human side." He is convinced his grandfather's insomnia stemmed from the fact that "his real life was so different from his yearnings for closeness to God and to his family...which seemed to elude him. [He] was only a poor parson that had difficulty with everyone he loved."

For those who might have a view of Calvin as "a hard man," John Randall answers that they never "traveled the deserts and mountains with him as I did. I bet they never saw him hold an entire congregation in the palm of his hand. I did." His grandson cherishes the time he spent with his grandfather roaming New Mexico, Arizona, Utah, and Colorado, visiting trading posts along the way, affording the elder man time and space to record his observations in his famous Log Books.

In later years Ross Calvin had gained weight and became noticeably fleshy. (Ross Calvin Papers, Center for Southwest Research, University Libraries, University of New Mexico)

Calvin's retirement was marked by his third and last marriage, ending at his death. From family accounts, this marriage was quite unlike those with Adine and Grace. Those were characterized by intense, reciprocated love terminated only by their deaths. Grandson John Randall believes his grandfather's marriage to Iris Pearle Legg on March 20, 1966, was more for "intellectual stimulation" as well as companionship. Both partners were older with considerable experience of life. Iris was four months away from her seventy-fourth birthday. He was some two and a half years her senior. She had a college education, had once taught school in Dallas, and had traveled widely in Latin America with her first husband, Aubrey Stewart Legg, a power company executive who died before she moved to Albuquerque. John Randall remembers her as cultured and something of a "grande dame" with an interest in books and learning. At the time of her marriage to Calvin, she was employed at Kirkland Air Force Base in Albuquerque and was attending the Episcopal Church, following her lifelong faith. That is undoubtedly where the two met and began seeing each other.

Ross Calvin and third wife Iris Pearle Legg Calvin in his study in Albuquerque. His last book *Barnabas in Pittsburgh* is at corner of desk. (Ross Calvin Papers, Center for Southwest Research, University Libraries, University of New Mexico)

Iris outlived Calvin by sixteen years. She remained in Albuquerque another eight following his death. Among her final obligations to her late husband was donating his papers to the University of New Mexico in March 1970. With his affairs in order, Iris moved to Oklahoma City. She spent her final years there in an area nursing home and died in Mercy Hospital on June 30, 1986. With her first husband she had shared ownership of a drugstore in McGregor, Texas, and it was her wish to be buried there. The rector of St. Paul's Episcopal Church of Waco performed her funeral service, and she was interred in the McGregor Cemetery. It may (or may not be) significant that the name "Calvin" does not appear on her gravestone.

Iris's donation of Calvin's papers to the Center for Southwest Research and Special Collections carried out his longtime, strongly held wish. Calvin had often expressed a desire to be remembered, albeit on his terms. His edited correspondence and other documents attest to that. In an Autumn 1965 essay for the *New Mexico Quarterly*, he remarked that his papers would have "no readers for the first century or two; but anything, if preserved long enough will interest the archaeologists who rediscover it and then write an introduction and notes for it." He added wryly, "I should know!" He was way off in his calculation. The first study of his importance appeared only seven years after his death.

He had other things to occupy his days in the years preceding his death, including resuming a voluminous correspondence, traveling to Europe and the Holy Land, and strengthening ties to his beloved alma mater. In 1959, he served as Albuquerque president of the Harvard-Yale-Princeton Club. Calvin reminded members their speaker would be Dr. Norris Bradbury, director of the Los Alamos Scientific Laboratory and, like him, a fellow holder of an honorary doctorate of laws from the University of New Mexico. Calvin had been cited by the university as "a distinguished clergyman," "able scholar," and "nationally recognized author." The citation pointed out that through his books Calvin had interpreted "with beauty and authenticity" the cultural patterns and heritage of the Southwest.

He was inordinately proud of his Harvard association, but that did not prevent him from writing the *Harvard Alumni Bulletin* chastising the school because he thought "Harvard has lost its position as a great institution of learning." He went on to say, "I do not see how it can regain its place without a complete reversal of recent faculty decisions." Calvin was echoing beliefs of a friend and fellow alumnus who was convinced the university was "appeasing the anarchists" by some of its administrative-faculty decisions.

Health problems intruded. Calvin's declining years were marked by concerns from friends, even if Calvin himself seldom voiced them. In early January 1966, just four years before Calvin's death, the University of New Mexico Press director, Roland Dickey, wrote to Lawrence Clark Powell in Tucson: "Worried a bit about Ross. Seems to be doing well [but] occasional memory lapses, fumbling for words...must be frustrating [for him]." Calvin had written several years earlier of a "mysterious illness" that had beset him on a visit with Powell when the latter was still at UCLA. Calvin had required hospitalization and believed it might have been a stroke: "Today it is exactly the anniversary of the day of that stroke that ruined me. Maybe I've never told you about it. I was never paralyzed by it, I can walk as well as always, but, oh, the forgetfulness that it causes me!"

Then, Calvin's relations with Rodney began fluctuating again. Seven letters, from January 30 through September 17, 1969, survive as testimony of a mysterious tension now impossible to elucidate. During the exchange Calvin reminds his son and his daughter-in-law of their last visit on April 15, 1968, and accuses him: "All contact ended with you on that date.... [I]t appears you no longer wish to communicate with me." That theme, mingled with talk of changing his will, permeates the rest of his correspondence. On June 10, Rodney admitted he had been "remiss in not writing." It is a newsy letter, including information that he and Christine had moved back to the old home in Littleton, Colorado, the sixteenth move of their marriage. He ended, "I love you Dad, tho I have 'erred and strayed like lost sheep'; this does not change my feelings for you. *Please know this.*" After underlining the last sentence, he concluded, "All my love, always, Rodney." Calvin wrote September 17, telling Rodney he was removing his name from his will. "I want to leave money to your children but not to you." He ended, "If this should be a final word between us, it is only because you desire it." The older man provided a way out: "At your own wish, you can still be, as always, my son." There is no record of further letters.

As he approached his end, Calvin seems to have felt the distance between his sons and himself ever more keenly. In one undated letter to his grandchildren, Calvin alluded to "a great gulf" between them and their grandparents, not of "their making nor yet completely of ours." John Randall Calvin recalls his grandfather being "sweet and tender" toward his grandchildren but never hugging Rodney. He sums up that the fallout of all this for the family was "horrendous."

Incongruity surrounded Calvin's last days as well. A lingering, uneasy, and restive death claimed him on January 30, 1970, at age eighty. He was then in an Albuquerque nursing facility, where he had gone when Iris could no longer cope, the once proud man having to be spoon fed. Charles remembers, "My father has told me several times, using the same phrase, that [Dr. Calvin] died 'cursing God.'" By all accounts his was a lonely passing. Iris visited, and Rodney came down from Colorado when he could. Peggy lived in Albuquerque and saw her father more often. But when the end came, Iris had gone home for the night, and no one was at his bedside when he died. He had outlived his beloved Adine by more than five decades. Grace had been gone ten years.

Calvin had never turned his back on acclaim. The relatively scant public notice paid his death would not have measured up to his expectations. His passing merited eight-column-inch obituaries in Albuquerque's two newspapers, the larger circulation, independently owned morning *Albuquerque Journal* and the afternoon Scripps-Howard *Albuquerque Tribune*. One account has his age wrong. They differ about where he died, one saying in a hospital. The *Journal* found it more interesting that Calvin was the father of Mrs. Edward V. Balcomb, wife of the Bernalillo County Commissioner and herself a prominent local socialite. Calvin was interred in Albuquerque's Fairview Memorial Cemetery February 2, 1970, where many of the city's elite have been buried over the years. That would have pleased him.

This photo of Ross Calvin Jr. was taken in Denver at age 73. (Calvin Family)

Ross Calvin Jr. is pictured just before his 97th birthday. (Calvin Family)

The Golden Eye is a 57-foot steel sloop John Randall Calvin and his wife Christina Louisa sailed in their circumnavigation of the globe. Here Calvin is at the helm off British Columbia, Canada. (John Randall Calvin)

Adine Chilton's family had this marker erected for the joint resting place of their daughter who died in 1918 and her husband Ross Calvin. He was buried in Albuquerque. (Ross Calvin Papers, Center for Southwest Research, University Libraries, University of New Mexico)

The final resting place for Ross R. Calvin is in Albuquerque's Fairview Memorial Park Cemetery. (Calvin Family)

Descendants of Ross Randall Calvin

Ross Randall Calvin was born on November 22, 1889, in Edgar County, Illinois, the son of Charles Fletcher Calvin and Addie Virginia Propst. He died on January 30, 1970, in Albuquerque, New Mexico. He married Olive Adine Chilton on June 12, 1917, in Pittsburgh, Pennsylvania. She was born on April 2, 1890, in Badger, Ind., the daughter of Charles Franklin Chilton and Adda Jane Myers. She died on December 18, 1918, in Pittsburgh. He married Grace Van Deurs Hance on January 28, 1925, in Pittsburgh. She was born on August 2, 1899, in Philadelphia, Pennsylvania, the daughter of Oscar Tibbals Hance and Sarah Jennie Roe. She died on January 21, 1961, in Las Vegas, New Mexico. He married Iris Pearle Robertson Legg on March 20, 1966, in Albuquerque. She was born on July 17, 1892, in Willow Springs, Missouri, the daughter of George Albert Robertson and Mary Anne Dollins. She was the widow of Aubrey Stewart Legg. She died on June 30, 1986, in Oklahoma City, Oklahoma.

Children

Ross Randall Calvin and Olive Adine Chilton had the following child:

Ross Randall Calvin Jr. was born on May 31, 1918, in Lafayette, Indiana He married Rosemary Clarke on September 17, 1941, in Hannibal, Missouri. He married Dorothy Ruth Leonhardt on June 21, 1947, in Evanston, Illinois. She was born on August 17, 1919, in Chicago, Illinois, the daughter of Paul Augustus Leonhardt and Ruth Myrtle Stark. She died on April 3, 1971, in Los Alamos, New Mexico.

Ross Randall Calvin and Grace Van Deurs Hance had the following children:

Rodney Provoost Calvin was born on January 7, 1926, in Geneva, New York. He died on March 19, 1987, in Green Valley, Arizona. He married Christine Gloria Templeton on June 11, 1950, in Albuquerque. She was the daughter of J. P. and Florence Templeton. She died in March 2015. He married Donna Justice on May 17, 1970.

Margaret Van Deurs Calvin was born on October 15, 1930, in Silver City, New Mexico. She died on November 29, 2006, in Albuquerque. She married Edward Vail Balcomb on August 6, 1950. He was born on August 9, 1923, in Albuquerque, the son of Kenneth Chester Balcomb and Kathryn Wise Johnson. He died on December 8, 2013, in Albuquerque.

Grandchildren

Ross Randall Calvin Jr. and Dorothy Ruth Leonhardt had the following children:

Charles David Calvin was born in 1948 in Evanston, Illinois. He married Nancy Pearl Bigbee in 1968 in Santa Fe, New Mexico. She was born in 1947 in Santa Fe, the daughter of Harry Long Bigbee and Sarah Elizabeth Roe. He married Inga Evelyn Clayton in 1983 in Denver, Colorado. She was born in 1955 in Fort Carson, Colorado, the daughter of Charles W. Clayton and Marianne M. Hausmann.

Virginia Anne Calvin was born in 1950 in Evanston, Ilinois. She married Michael Peter Jacobs in 1983 in Seattle, Washington. He was born in 1955 in Seattle, the son of Gerald Haliday Jacobs and Eva Marie Lecompte.

Mary Susan Calvin was born in 1951 in Evanston, Illinois. She married Mark Thistlethwaite in 1971 in Phoenix, Arizona. He was born in 1943 in Fort Lauderdale, Florida, the son of Robert E. and Elizabeth Thistlethwaite. He died in 2005 in Las Vegas, Nevada. She married Robert

Ames Bruner in 1989 in Northbrook, Illinois. He was born in 1943 in New Orleans, Louisiana, the son of Claude Douglas Bruner and Lillie Amparo Edmiston.

John Richard Calvin was born in 1952 in Los Alamos, New Mexico. He married Virginia Lea Williams in 1970 in Amarillo, Texas. She was born in 1953 in Albuquerque. He married Julie Miller in 1975 in Denver, Colo. He married Leslie Witherspoon in 1983 in Denver. She was born in 1952. He married Ellen Serine Grothe in 1998 in Seattle, Washington. She was born in 1958 in Lisbon, North Dakota, the daughter of Kenneth Grothe and Charlene Anderson.

Thomas Phillip Calvin was born in 1957 in Los Alamos, New Mexico. He married Linda Kay Daniel in 1985 in Albuquerque. She was born in 1961 in Albuquerque, the daughter of William B. Daniel and Barbara Lawson.

Rodney Provoost Calvin and Christine Templeton had the following children:

John Randall Calvin was born in 1953. He married Elizabeth Roop in 1978. He married Christina Louisa Viggiano in 2004. She was born in 1951 in Veneto, Italy.

Cynthia M. Calvin was born in 1955. She married Eugene (Mac) McShane in 1987.

Edward Masterson Calvin was born in 1961 in Farmington, New Mexico. He married Kristie Lynn Kabance in 2004. She was born in Denver, Colorado.

Edward Vail Balcomb and Margaret Van Deurs Calvin had the following children:

Teresa Vail Balcomb was born in 1952 in Albuquerque. She married James Robert Tyron.

Charlotte Victoria Balcomb was born in 1956 in Albuquerque. She married Wilkie Degiampietro (Peter) Lane.

Great-grandchildren

Charles David Calvin and Nancy Pearl Bigbee had the following child:

> Anne Marie Calvin was born in 1972 in New Haven, Connecticut. She married Richard James Ference in 2002 in Sedona, Arizona. He was born in 1958 in Charleston, South Carolina, the son of Victor James Ference and Joan Margaret Skocik.

Michael Peter Jacobs and Virginia Anne Calvin had the following children:

> Alana Jacobs Calvin was born in 1985 in Seattle, Wash. She married Mark Le in 2013 in Tacoma, Washington. He is the son of Hung Le and Cuc Nguyen.
>
> Nicolas Calvin Jacobs was born in 1987 in Seattle, Washington.

Robert Ames Bruner and Mary Susan Calvin had the following children:

> Richard Calvin Bruner was born in 1990 in Evanston, Illinois.
>
> Joseph Calvin Bruner was born in 1993 in Evanston, Illinois.

Thomas Phillip Calvin and Linda Kay Daniel had the following children:

> John Isaac Calvin was born in 1992 in Kent, Washington.
>
> Angelina Rose Calvin was born in 1996 in Kent, Washington.

John Randall Calvin and Elizabeth Roop had the following children:

> Ross Way Calvin was born in 1982 in Denver, Colorado.
>
> Clayton Way Calvin was born in 1991 in Denver, Colorado.

Edward Masterson Calvin and Kristie Lynn Kabance had the following children:

> Courtney Rae Calvin was born in 2009 in Denver, Colorado.
>
> Connor James Calvin was born in 2012 in Denver, Colorado.

James Robert Tyron and Teresa Vail Balcomb had the following children:

> Elyce Balcomb Tyron was born in 1983 in Fort Worth, Texas. She married Sean Patrick Sheehan in 2011. He was born in 1981 in Albuquerque.
>
> Connor Boyle Tyron was born in 1985 in Los Angeles, California. He married Carolina Ponce Orellana in 2013. She was born in 1981 in Guayaquil, Ecuador.

Peter Lane and Charlotte Balcomb had the following children:

> Spencer Vail Lane was born in 1993 in Orlando, Florida
>
> Ansel Edward Lane was born in 1996 in Albuquerque, New Mexico.

Great-great-grandchildren

Richard James Ference and Anne Marie Calvin had the following child:

> Charles Victor Ference was born in 2007 in Scottsdale, Arizona.

Mark Le and Alana Jacobs Calvin had the following child:

> Olivia Grace Le was born 2015 in Tacoma, Washington.

Notes and Sources

Throughout this section, in order to set Ross Randall Calvin off from the other Calvins, I refer to him as RRC.

For my research, papers held at two archives have been indispensable. The Center for Southwest Research and Special Collections at the University of New Mexico, under the always kind and valuable guidance of Chris Geherin, has the single largest collection of material on RRC extant: the Ross Calvin Papers, 1889–1969. The Institute of Historical Survey Foundation (IHSF) in Mesilla Park, New Mexico, holds official correspondence between RRC and his bishops when he was a serving priest in the Missionary District of New Mexico and Southwest Texas of the Episcopal Church in Silver City and Clovis, New Mexico.

My book has greatly benefitted from the valuable input of a trio of Calvin's grandchildren: John Randall (Rodney's son), Charles (Ross Jr.'s oldest son), and Mary (Ross Jr.'s younger daughter). Mary furnished a descendants chart of the Ross R. Calvin family as well as a biographical sketch of her great-grandfather. Every family should have someone like her to gather and preserve the leaves of their life. Charles offered many of his own and his father's insights. John Randall did the same. As with any of us, their perceptions were based on memories, experiences, and disparate views. In addition, Mary and Charles are the proofreaders every writer wants.

I am grateful to Joy Morehouse Carlson and her husband Neal for lending me *A Mystical Bride* and granting permission to quote from and reproduce it. This beautiful little book was passed down to her from her grandfather, James Otis Chilton, Adine's first cousin. It not only represents a remarkable keepsake but offers a valuable insight as well into RRC's heart and mind at the tragic loss of his young bride. It also reveals a spiritual dimension never shown in any of his surviving writings, as far as I know. Ross Jr. also had a copy as did Rodney; thus the book was not preserved only by Adine's relatives. Although RRC destroyed many papers he considered private, he liked "to display his humanity," notes a family member, who feels a *Mystical Bride* is "evidence" of this. He believes a more mature RRC "must have" wanted others to see the booklet. Although RRC might have thought the book "overly sentimental or even maudlin," he notes the book "certainly" presented his human dimension.

Repeated interviews with family members nuanced my understanding of family dynamics. Some members of the family loved him, and some definitely did not. I hope I have been fair to everyone concerned. RRC as a person was, by all evidence, complex, complicated, contradictory. After pondering my decision long and hard, I felt strongly that he needed to be presented warts and all in order to give due homage to his remarkable descendants, rather than shoving the more unsavory portions of his biography under the metaphorical rug.

In writing this book, I am indebted to Professor L. G. Moses of Oklahoma State University. Dr. Moses wrote an essay on RRC: "If There Be Sermons in Stones, I Have Not Heard Them," *Historical Magazine of the Episcopal Church* 46: 2 (1977): 333–47. I often returned to his graceful narrative for guidance and inspiration. My book is better because of his ideas and insights. He served as a touchstone throughout. Lawrence Clark Powell wrote often of RRC as he discoursed on the literature of the New Mexico and the Southwest, especially in his acclaimed *Southwest Classics* (see below). One item I referred to often is a six-page typed list entitled "Papers and articles 115," beginning in 1930 and going through 1966 of apparently *everything* RRC wrote in those years.

Dr. D. Wayne Gunn has been a mentor since the time I was pursuing my graduate degrees, but more importantly always a friend. I have tried to bear in mind his stricture to make my writing as graceful as possible. Dr. Gunn was a sounding board throughout the writing stage, offering solid advice and suggestions and then became an editor of the manuscript in the truest sense of the term. My praise would be even more effusive if he would permit it, but I owe him a huge debt for making this book what it is.

Dr. Richard Melzer and Sunny Yates deserve special thanks for their meticulous attention to detail in the manuscript and for saving me from myself. Hearty thanks too to Meredith D. Dodge and Royce Grubic for editing and to friends and readers Dave Oram, Dick Thompson, and George Muncrief. My manuscript benefited hugely from their numerous "good catches" in proofing. Royce supplied a bibliography, which provides much of the material used in the "Sources" section. Public Services Librarian Simon Elliott of the UCLA Special Collections pitched in at the last minute to provide a much-needed photo of Lawrence Clark Powell. Chellee Chase also performed her usual computer wizardry. In the end, of course, any errors or oversights that remain are mine.

Jim Smith of Sunstone Press showed faith in this project even after I myself once gave up on it. My wife Peggy stood by me throughout and endured endless trips to Albuquerque and lonely hours in hotel rooms while I prowled the Center for Southwest Research, especially and exhaustively Box 6 with numerous items, old business records, letters, and clippings. Ross Jr. provided photos and supported acquisition of others when help was needed.

Photographs

There are four principal sources for the photographs used in this book. Through the generosity of the Center for Southwest Research, the majority come from the Calvin Papers. The Calvin family is next, followed by the Institute of Historical Research Foundation by arrangement, and lastly DePauw University's yearbook, *Mirage*. Some of the Calvin family photographs were from slides taken by Ross Jr., who also made a financial contribution to enable use of additional photographs held by the Institute of Historical Research Foundation.

Chapter 1: Learning Beckons

The comment concerning "the incredible double-barreled surname" comes from the Moses essay, but I've seen it in RRC's own writing too. RRC would have liked people to believe his side of the family descended from the famed theologian John Calvin, but there is no evidence of this. One reference to the "incredible" Luther Calvin name comes from a brief biographical sketch RRC wrote on June 25, 1962.

Mary Calvin furnished me a copy of the sketch RRC wrote about his father.

RRC always referred to his journals and field notes as "Log Books" although those writing about him sometimes joined the two words into one. There were seven volumes.

Sometime around 1955, in an untitled essay, RRC wrote his recollections of his earliest introduction to the formal study of botany at Chrisman High School in 1905. He had begun keeping a herbarium by that time. It took him thirty-five years, he confessed, to identify one of the specimens he had collected and kept in it, *Hydrophyllum macophyllum*.

Material about RRC's youth in Chrisman, Illinois, was furnished by the Edgar County Genealogical Society in Paris, Illinois, Linda Cary and Joyce Brown, co-directors. They provided newspaper clippings from the *Chrisman Weekly Courier* concerning RRC's high school days and early courtship of Adine Chilton. The touching "Letter to Santa" letter from Ross Jr. and RRC's one-year birthday note to his son (see below) came from the *Courier* as well.

Background for RRC's undergraduate years at DePauw University came from three sources: *Mirage*, the university yearbooks for 1910 and 1911; the website *DePauw University: A Pictorial History*; and Linda V. Butler, Archives Assistant at the DePauw Archives. George B. Manhart's two-volume, 596-page *DePauw through the Ages* (Greencastle, Ind.: DePauw University Press, 1962) is exhausting in its detail. The yearbooks include photographs of Ross and Adine along with information on their club and society memberships. RRC was a member of the track team; their picture is the only one of him not in street clothes or graduation regalia.

To get a broader sense of student life at Harvard during the period RRC was there, I consulted writings that discussed T. S. Eliot's, John Dos Passos's, and E. E. Cummings's Harvard years: Lyndall Gordon's *Elliot's Early Years* (Oxford: Oxford University Press, 1977); George J. Becker's *John Dos Passos* (New York: Frederick Unger, 1974); Charles D. Bernardin's "John Dos Passos' Harvard Years," *The New England Quarterly*, March 1954; Virginia Spencer Carr's *Dos Passos; A Life* (Garden City, New York: Doubleday, 1984); and Adam Kirsch's "The Rebellion of E. E. Cummings," *Harvard Magazine*, March-April 2005. Samuel Eliot Morrison's *Three Centuries of Harvard* (Cambridge, Mass.: Harvard University Press, 1965) contains information about the university's growth and change of direction during RRC's days there as a graduate student, but it offers surprisingly little about student life.

Chapter 2: A Love Lost, A New Family Begun

As L. G. Moses tells us, RRC found time during his first semester at Carnegie Tech to write and submit to *Atlantic Monthly* a short story that he called "The Last Sunset." Set in ancient Rome, the story was loosely based on *Romeo and Juliet*. In rejecting his efforts, the editor wrote, "We have found that to breathe the breath of life once more into a classical story is one of the most difficult of literary problems."

RRC was deeply in love, and everything he wrote to and about Adine reveals it. His love letters certainly do. *A Mystical Bride* is the ultimate tribute. Although RRC otherwise tended to keep his sentimental side to himself, among his papers at the Center for Southwest Research is an index of Adine's letters to him. The earliest was June 11, 1910, and the last June 9, 1917.

Charles Calvin first related the story of his grandfather's reasons for his conversion to Episcopalism in a telephone conversation March 30, 2015, and clarified my understanding in a meeting September 13, 2015. Charles said his father, Ross Jr., believed the very last basis upon which one should choose religious beliefs was for its adherents. Although his mother was a Baptist, RRC disparaged them, calling them "Holy Rollers."

Details of the wedding are provided by L. G. Moses. Information about the newlyweds' honeymoon stay at the Hotel Martinique comes from RRC's Log Book. The hostelry is now the Radisson Martinique on Broadway in New York City. RRC would be shocked at the room rate increase. With luck he might get a room today for $175-$200. What he paid for their room *might* suffice for the doorman's tip.

RRC's admiration for Adine's teaching skills comes from the column-length obituary of her in the *Chrisman Weekly Courier*, January 3, 1919. No authorship is attributed, but no one other than RRC could have written it.

The touching account of Adine's illness, her death, and her funeral comes from *A Mystical Bride* (Pittsburgh, Pennsylvania: Arsenal Printing Company, 1919). RRC was just twenty-nine; not until he was sixty-eight would he again write something so private. It is in stark contrast to how he felt later about anything touching on his personal life; tellingly, it is not included in an exhaustive list of his writings he compiled just four years before his death.

RRC's stricture about guarding his privacy was no more evident than in a December 5, 1949, letter to Ross Jr. and his wife, Dorothy, admonishing them to make certain his mother's papers were destroyed. In accordance with his wishes, most, but not all, were. RRC's widow, in keeping with his wishes, deposited only those papers he wished preserved with the Center for Southwest Research in March 1970.

RRC expressed his lack of fear about contracting the Spanish flu in an article in the Church of the Ascension Bulletin, January 5, 1919.

The following is from Charles Calvin (email, December 27, 2014): "Rodney told me about the rubber hose [incident] during a conversation in Fort Lupton,

[Colorado]." I also have a similar account from someone who does not wished to be quoted.

Charles (telephone interview, March 30, 2014) supplied the description of how a young, newly-wed Grace might have reacted to Ross Jr.'s being introduced into her Geneva household. Charles and I met for the first time in Santa Fe on September 13, 2015; he enlarged upon his thoughts then, leading me to reflect on how important it is to consider the context of any action to the fullest. The account of failed attempts at assimilation into the Geneva family, as well as the lake incident, comes from Ross Jr.'s recollections passed on to Charles (telephone interview, October 12, 2014), modified in comments on October 29, 2015. The letter from father to son Charles thinks is "more human and affectionate" than any other communication from RRC he can recall (email, January 20, 2015).

Ross Jr. never accepted that his father's learning and the number of degrees were superior to his own. Charles (personal interview, September 13, 2015) believes his father always felt "he was every bit the man of words" as was his father because both shared a love of learning. Charles says his father did not aspire to be literary, but chose his words more to communicate than to impress (email Oct. 28, 2015). Ross Jr. was an excellent speller and was offended that Charles would dare call his girlfriend to verify a spelling of a word rather than accept his rendering. The older man had spelled it correctly. Both RRC and Ross Jr. "were passionate" about learning," concluded Charles.

Ross Jr.'s "Santa letter" appeared in the *Chrisman Weekly Courier* of December 20, 1923.

Charles (telephone interview, October 12, 2014) is the source of the idea of the father-son relationship never being far from the family's minds, and that it is not "a comfortable one." John Randall Calvin says even today he feels "outrage" at Ross Jr.'s treatment at his grandfather's hands. He shared those and other feelings quietly and matter-of-factly in an interview in his lovely Casa Rondeña Winery on a beautiful New Mexico fall morning in Los Ranchos, October 1, 2013. He was the first of the Calvin family with whom I spoke.

The original of RRC's birthday letter to his son comes from Ernest Dudley Chase, Boston, Massachusetts. Ross Senior presumably wrote the note around the child's May 31 birthday. The Chase Papers are now in the National Museum of American History in Washington, DC.

John Randall Calvin (email, September 11, 2015) feels his grandfather was "clearly sensitive and loving" although his outward persona might have shown him to be "a hard man." He thinks his grandfather was "somehow tortured in many ways." That, he thinks, "kept him out of his touch with his more human side." RRC's love letters to his first two wives clearly demonstrate his warm side although he had distinctly different ways of addressing them. In a February 17, 1917, letter to Adine he calls her "My heart's beloved." With Grace, written on Good Shepherd letterhead July 26, 1927, he takes a much more informal tone, calling her "Sweetie dearest," telling her how much he misses her, saying "it sure is lonesome here without you and the 'little feller' [Rodney]." He closes, "God keep you both, Sweetie! I love you. R." The occasion for the letter is puzzling. The Calvins had arrived in Silver City in early January 1927, and soon after he is writing her expressing his loneliness. Had she returned east for a summer visit after only a few months in New Mexico? Mary Calvin is the source of the story that Grace's uncle Gouverneur Provoost Hance sent money to visit him every other year at St. Barnabas House in Pittsburgh. Some of those biennial excursions obviously later included everyone. Once in the East, other visits and excursions would have been possible. Photos show RRC, Grace, and the children at the beach, presumably the New Jersey shore.

The Cerro Grande Fire of May 2000 began as a controlled burn and ended with some three hundred families losing their homes as the inferno consumed about 47,000 acres.

The information about RRC's children Rodney and Peggy "knowing to stay out" of his office when the door was closed comes from the late Edward V. Balcolm, Peggy's husband, in an interview in Belen, New Mexico, on December 13, 2012. Ed died a year later. He was a great source of information, and I wish I could have used more of his stories. An example: When RRC, Grace, and baby Rodney came to Silver City, "she brought with her an entire trunk of baby food" for the child. Her new home was not the outpost she thought it was, however: "She learned Silver City had grocery stores." Here is one from RRC's Clovis days: "[He] didn't mind a drink. I'd bring him a fifth of whiskey from Albuquerque because Clovis was in the Bible Belt." Still another: "In the wet/dry elections [RRC was a "wet"] the temperance people would set up a tent outside his church with loudspeakers blaring [religious music] to drown out his services." Ed told me RRC's "most affluent" parishioners" were "the town's bootleggers." He added that RRC learned to "identify with such people." This assessment is backed up by RRC's own recollections of his affinity with prisoners, the down-and-out, mining men, ranchers, CCC enrollees, and others.

Chapter 3: Leaving the "Known World": The Silver City Years

Ross Jr. wrote about not accompanying his family to Silver City in an essay "Human versus Divine Wisdom," July 1, 2004. Although I did not read it, his daughter Mary relayed the gist of it. As a result of not going west, the elder son formed an even stronger attachment to his Chrisman grandparents and viewed them as surrogate parents, especially grandmother Addie. Despite this, Ross Jr.'s "entire life involved a yearning" to establish a "warming up" with his father. As his son Charles puts it, Ross Jr. felt that "consanguinity alone ought to have been a basis for relationship."

My description of the Silver City railroad station as RRC and his family might have seen it is based on a wonderful poster issued as part of the 2010 New Mexico Heritage Preservation Month series from a photograph taken by Waldo Twitchell around 1920. Twitchell's photo was made available by the Palace of Governors Photo Archives (NMHM/DCA) #51083. The scene would not have changed much in the seven years between when this photo was taken and when the Calvins arrived in Silver City. This is not the only "word picture" I draw based on photos I came across during my research. I do the same several times in this chapter in describing Rodney and Peggy based on photos taken by their parents and contained in a photo album donated by Peggy to the Institute of Historical Survey Foundation. I love the old photos preserved by archives and hope those who love history will do their best to support such institutions. Archivists will be among the first folks in heaven, but they won't let you in without your cotton gloves.

RRC is quoted many times and in many places saying that he anticipated staying in New Mexico only a few months until his throat ailment was resolved. An undated index card note at the Institute of Historical Survey Foundation indicates he was transferred (licensed out) of the Diocese of Western New York on December 31, 1926, but that his transfer was not received by the Missionary District of New Mexico and Southwest Texas until February 23, 1928. Edward Balcolm (interview, December 13, 2012) raised the question, "Is there anything more worthless than a preacher who can't talk?"

John Randall Calvin (interview, October 1, 2014) suggested that the stress his grandfather put upon himself to accomplish all that he did contributed to his insomnia. Ernie Pyle thought the same. John Randall is the source of all the quotations concerning his grandfather, provided in a series of telephone calls, personal interviews, and emails on September 9, 2013, October 1 and 4, 2013,

February 5 and 19, 2015, and September 11 and 15, 2015. One was even sent from his fifty-seven foot steel sloop *Golden Eye* as he and his wife were bound for New Zealand during their three-year multi-stage circumnavigation of the globe.

The Grant County (New Mexico) Clerk's Office allowed me free access to its bound copies to copy RRC's "Village Parson" columns from the *Silver City Daily Press* and stories about him in the *Silver City Independent*.

RRC always promoted his books and photographic work, most of which grew out of his field trips to gather material for his botanical studies and later his articles and books. An example of his entrepreneurship is a tastefully printed note of November 30, 1935, advertising "The Rector Pictures," an upcoming exhibition at the Philipps Gift Shop in Silver City's El Sol Theater Building. I gained the impression Grace's pictures were sometimes shown there as well. One of his photos, he wrote in the note, shows "a high mountain meadow at one edge of which rise two towering spruces while at the other stands an aspen tree through whose golden foliage the sun is shining." He added, "I think you will enjoy seeing them." One article reflecting his interest in photography is "Considering the Beginner." He wrote ten such pieces for the magazine between 1926 and 1930. In "The Parson" in the *Silver City Enterprise* of February 1942 RRC said he had always considered the camera "a recorder, not a picture-maker."

Thomas O'Connor of Lake Oswego, Oregon, wrote a graduate paper for a history class at the University of New Mexico in 1971 on "Ross Calvin: New Mexican Naturalist," from which comes the quote about RRC's seeking release in nature from a troubled world. O'Connor kindly poked around his attic one evening until he found the essay to share with me.

On June 6, 1938, RRC wrote of the lessons that could be learned from a clump of raw earth. He credited Silver City housewife Mrs. McAnulty for bringing a ball of dirt containing "a curious orange and brown flower" to him for identification.

John Randall Calvin conveyed an observation of his grandfather's views of the less fortunate in an interview October 4, 2013. One particularly acerbic newspaper comment to the contrary can be found in RRC's *Silver City Daily Press* "Village Parson" column of April 22, 1933.

In "Ministrations in the C.C.C. Camps" appeared in the *Silver City Enterprise* August 11, 1933, RRC identifies himself as the "Co-ordinating Chaplain," indicating there was more than one. In keeping with the program's philosophy, administrators of all stripes seemed to be paid at least something for their services, so it is reasonable to assume RRC earned a modest stipend. One thing that struck

RRC about the "woodpeckers" (a commonly used affectionate name for the CCC enrollees), besides their poor Sunday school attendance (he offered a trophy for the best turnout, but it didn't help), was their "funny hats." A plaque with a photo marking the site of one camp is at the Little Walnut Picnic Grounds just north of Silver City. I see it often while walking my dog, Smokie. Their hats don't seem all that funny to either of us. New Mexico historian Richard Melzer has written of the CCC in New Mexico in his insightful book *Coming of Age in the Great Depression: The Civilian Conservation Corps Experience in New Mexico, 1933-1942* (Las Cruces, New Mexico.: Yucca Tree Press, 2000). He noted that RRC was pleased that "appreciative enrollees responded to his [nature] lectures with hearty applause." As always, RRC was especially concerned for and tried to befriend those CCC "woodpeckers" who seemed destined to go "down the lonesome road that leads to the penitentiary door." *Mr. Fairchild Sleeps* is to be found in Box 5, The Center for Southwest Research.

"Thinking Toward the Future" appeared in *New Mexico Magazine*, November 1932. In point of fact, the state currently ranks near the bottom or midway by every measure of success from student achievement to per capita income. It a different story when considering such factors as teenage pregnancy, drug abuse, and crime— all tied to disparities in education and income. Then the state occupies an unwanted ranking at or near the top.

RRC described his work for the Soil Conservation Service in *The Silver City Enterprise* on December 12, 1934. Eight years later, on August 4, 1942, RRC wrote Russell Lord, editor of the influential *The Land* magazine his view that "soil conservation is not dead—just dormant." Money spent on conservation in the Southwest, he added, was "not wasted." He noted changes in agricultural practices brought on by more modern methods and improved production, even in dry years, and observed that "change was not climatic, but economic." By then he was living in Clovis, where farming was much more predominant than in the ranchland around Silver City. RRC contributed five articles to *The Land*. The title of one predated the advent of Walmart by twenty years but seemed prescient of the decline of the American small town: "Goodbye Main Street," July 1942.

RRC wrote about his stock losses in his Log Book, September 30, 1931. The long steady decline had begun in April of that year, and RRC was no more adept at extricating himself from the financial morass than anyone else.

Chapter 4: *Sky Determines*

Lois Dwight Cole wrote RRC's agent J. N. Masterton on September 28, 1933, thanking him for bringing the *Sky Determines* manuscript to Macmillan's Fifth Avenue offices in New York City and assuring him the editorial board had "read it carefully" and "discussed it at length." She then segued into her cost-sharing suggestion. She told Masterton she hoped he would inform her if RRC was interested so they "could proceed even further." Hers likely was the most important letter in RRC's literary career. The New York Public Library holds the Macmillan Company records 1889–1990, but they show no correspondence with RRC. The book was dedicated to his parents.

As noted in the text, there is a much to be said about the concept of determinism. I had known a bit about it before writing this book, but friend and fellow teacher Royce Grubic helped fill in gaps. For those wishing only a quick and easy-to-read summary, I refer them to the article by that title in Wikipedia. The idea of determinism remained with RRC throughout his writing career. In the Autumn 1965 issue of *New Mexico Quarterly* he wrote an article, "Man Determines." It represented a shift in subject, but the essay chiefly was concerned with interpretation and the role of an interpreter.

Silver City friend Tom Hester, who has taught and spoken on RRC before and after I began this book, graciously found time between his many volunteer duties to share his thoughts about the man and *Sky Determines*. We visited over coffee three times in November 2014.

As for RRC's prejudicial comments, they apparently persisted. When Thomas C. Donnelly requested an essay on New Mexico's people (see below), he told RRC the state's natives "don't like to be called 'poverty-stricken.'" Some of them, he added, are "rather violent" on the subject. Donnelly suggested using the phrase "economic difficulties" instead to describe their plight.

Chapter 5: The Book's Reception

On September 9, 1941, RRC wrote Macmillan asking the publisher to "kindly send...six copies of my book...and charge same to my account." He asked Macmillan to estimate as closely as possible how many copies remained "in your stock. It isn't necessary to estimate how many copies are in the hands of your branches over the country. Just tell me how many copies you have on hand." I suspect there was a reason for the exactness of his query. He publicly said there would not be a new edition, but privately he wanted to do one, and having firm numbers may have been one way of laying the groundwork. In 1948 the University of New Mexico Press issued a second edition (without the subtitle) with illustrations by Peter Hurd; then in 1965 it brought out a revised and enlarged third edition. Most recently, in 1993, the High-Lonesome Press in Silver City published a facsimile edition of the second, 1948, edition. Peter Hurd (1904–1984) was a New Mexican painter whose "official" portrait of President Lyndon Johnson was angrily rejected by the sitter.

RRC enjoyed many laudatory reviews of *Sky Determines* in such prestigious publications as *The Times Literary Supplement*, September 13, 1934. His papers at the University of New Mexico contain the more important ones which someone (likely either he or Grace) meticulously retyped and annotated. There were no photocopy machines in 1934.

R. L. Duffus, author of *The Santa Fe Trail* (1930), wrote *The New York Times* review published on May 6, 1934, with the evocative title "The Land of Blooming Desert, Bright Sun and Little Rain." Duffus (1888–1972), like RRC, had a love for the outdoors. He was suited for his assignment by virtue of roaming the Vermont hills and mountains as a youth and then getting a quality education clear across the country at Stanford University before joining the *Times* editorial staff as an essayist, a post he held for thirty-two years. Duffus freely expressed in his review what New Mexico meant to him: "The value of New Mexico...is more psychological than material." About the only thing Duffus found fault with was RRC's insistence to "sell the state as a whole." To Duffus that was "as though some overzealous manager of a chamber of commerce contrived to edit an otherwise thoroughly charming piece of copy."

Eugene Manlove Rhodes (1869–1934) is another figure important to the literature of New Mexico who, like RRC, was born elsewhere but found inspiration after relocating. I've always considered him a semi-tragic figure because of the often poor condition of his finances and his health. New Mexico politician Albert Bacon Fall once gave Rhodes a house when he could no longer pay his rent in Alamogordo. Shortly after Rhodes's death, Calvin presented a paper entitled "Pasó por aqui" before the Southwestern Writers' Conference at what is now New Mexico Highlands University in Las Vegas, New Mexico. He revised it January 5, 1953. I have long admired Rhodes's short novel *Pasó por aqui*, and once, when I inquired about it at the Alamogordo Public Library, a nice lady there gave me a lovely reprint. The book takes its title from the carvings on New Mexico's famed Inscription Rock at El Morro by early New Mexico explorer Juan de Oñate of those "who passed this way." The Alamogordo library holds an extensive collection of Rhodes material. *A Bar Cross Man: The Life & Personal Writings of Eugene Manlove Rhodes* by W. H. Hutchinson (Norman, Oklahoma: University of Oklahoma Press, 1956) is a biography.

One would have thought *New Mexico Magazine* might have reached out to any one of a number of the state's outstanding writers then living in New Mexico for a polished, literate review. Erna and Harvey Fergusson, Edwin Corlee, Willa Cather, among many others could have fulfilled the assignment. The magazine might also have devoted more than eleven paragraphs in its May 1934 article. Predictably, because it promoted tourism for the entire state, the magazine complained that if *Sky Determines* had "one weakness" it was that the book was "limited to one area of the state [the southwest section] rather than covering the entire area." RRC must not have felt miffed; he contributed twenty-one articles to the magazine over a period of some thirty years.

The Royal Geographic Society's *Geographic Journal* review reappeared in Vol. 84, No. 5, November 1934. Its American Geographical Society counterpart followed in the *Geographic Review*, Vol. 25, No. 1, January 1935. The sociological review appeared in the *American Journal of Sociology*, Vol. 40, No. 4, January 1935. Someone in the Macmillan publicity machine was working the review possibilities for all they were worth.

Different in format and purpose yet contemporaneous with the 1934 newspaper reviews was Lester Raines's *Writers and Writing of New Mexico*, published by New Mexico Normal University (now New Mexico Highlands University). It is an 8½ x 11 inch, 142-page mimeographed booklet. It grew out of English Department round tables Raines had held. He devoted three pages to RRC. The Highlands University archives hold a copy.

RRC contributed the poem, "The Weavers," to *El Palacio Magazine* for its August 1930 issue.

Eight decades after its appearance, *Sky Determines* is still being warmly reviewed, but in a format RRC could not have envisioned—the Internet. On April 22, 2014, journalist and author John S. Sledge posted "A Southwestern Classic Turns Eighty" on *VQR Online*.

"Pueblenos" is the term RRC used for those Native American people residing in pueblos (Spanish for communities or villages) along the Rio Grande.

Chapter 6: The Book's Continuing Importance

For a scientific discussion of the meteorological-climatological dimensions of determinism the author is grateful for the generous input and lucid commentary of U.S. Weather Service professionals David Hefner and David J. Novlan of El Paso and Santa Teresa, New Mexico. Novlan began his first email to me on August 18, 2014, by noting, "It so happens as a Climatologist" that he had a copy of *Sky Determines* in his "personal library." He went on to say, "A lot can be said about that interesting book...." He then provided a closely-packed three and one half page "mini-lecture" that helped inform what I wrote about weather and climate and how RRC viewed its impact. Novlan explained how monsoons work and that in New Mexico we have three monsoon seasons instead of just the one most New Mexicans speak of. Hefner followed up August 19, 2014, with a long email that helped set straight some of RRC's ideas about how mountains serve as "weather breeders." He provided much more information as well. Because I had asked them to evaluate RRC's ideas and tell me if they had any relevance today, they freely did. Any misinterpretations of their comments are mine alone of course.

William deBuys lives among descendants of early settlers of rural northern New Mexico who have rediscovered the value of the land and the importance of holding onto it. *A Great Aridness*, *The Walk*, and *River of Traps* help tell his personal story. Gracious as always, despite teaching and administrative duties, Bill found time to offer valuable suggestions and ideas about development of this book.

My research took Peggy and me to Hillsboro, New Mexico, in the heart of the Black Range, an area RRC knew well, for a wintery lunchtime interview with Harley Shaw and his wife on January 20, 2014.

Sharman Apt Russell (email October 20, 2014) is a former teaching colleague whose opinions I value highly. Occupied as she was with her research and writing, Sharman found time to squeeze in her thoughtful insights about the contributions of RRC and *Sky Determines* to the Southwest literary landscape and its environment.

Allyson Siwik (emails, September 18 and October 27, 2014) is one of many who have been drawn to New Mexico through reading *Sky Determines* and then made their own contribution to the state. Allyson's husband still loves books; he owns a bookshop in downtown Silver City. Lyle Saunders, who reviewed the 1948 University of New Mexico edition, wrote in the Summer 1949 *New Mexico Quarterly*, "A good many years ago, I read on a series of warm summer afternoons a book which had a considerable influence on my subsequent behavior." Saunders concluded that the New Mexico RRC depicted was "the land for me." Subsequently, "I put my few affairs in order, burned my bridges, and in a 1928 Chevrolet, recently painted red, set out for Cibola."

Jim Norwine is as thoughtful a commentator on climate as I know. I knew he would offer penetrating insights on RRC's legacy, and he did in an email on January 2, 2015. For Tom Hester, see above.

M. L. Salmon is an author and co-owner with wife, Cherie, of High-Lonesome Books in Silver City, a press and a bookshop. Like so many others, "Dutch" went out of his way when I asked for help (telephone calls, September 9, 2014, and December 9, 2014). Someone (I don't remember who) once called him "a cult figure" for his *Gila Descending* (1986). His book calls up images for me of John Graves's *Goodbye to a River*. Salmon, a committed fly fisherman and courser of hounds, is an indefatigable fighter to keep the river free through his advocacy and activism.

Chapter 7: Lawrence Clark Powell, A Special Bond

Lawrence Clark Powell (1906–2001) wrote often of RRC. If I were to suggest any one of his works for the most comprehensive and insightful view it would be *Southwest Classics* (Los Angeles: Ritchie Press, 1974). Quotations throughout the chapter are taken principally, but not always, from it. Powell would have been twenty-eight when *Sky Determines* appeared and would have lacked a venue for a review. My view of what existed between the two men is purely subjective. I feel the bond, if that is what it truly was, was mostly one-sided. RRC wrote many times to Powell; if there was correspondence on Powell's side, I did not find it. My sense of Powell was that he was generous and kind and would not be deliberately mean-spirited. I would have liked to have known him.

The importance of Powell to RRC's self-esteem is undeniable. Here are just two examples to illustrate the point. On November 24, 1964, RRC wrote Patricia Manahan, editor of *Westways Magazine*, regarding a manuscript he had submitted for publication. RRC reminded Manahan that Powell had twice mentioned him in her magazine, referring to Powell's "notable comment." RRC said he did not know if his "prose style merits all his [Powell's] praise." Some two weeks later, RRC wrote Powell (December 10, 1964) appearing to feast again on everything good Powell had ever said about his work. He reminded Powell of his "forthright decisive" comments on *Sky Determines* and that only "ethics and/or good taste" restrained him (RRC) from distributing even more fliers with Powell's praise than he had. RRC at this time was lobbying the University of New Mexico publications board for a re-issue of *Sky Determines*. I have found nothing showing RRC's reaction to Powell's comments that he (RRC) had only one good book in him.

RRC wrote Lyle Saunders, who had been inspired to move to New Mexico after reading *Sky Determines* many years before, to thank him for his praise of his work. In his letter he referred to a "religious book I'm on working now [that] won't be [as good] as *Sky Determines*." There is no further reference to this "religious book," and the manuscript (perhaps unfinished) has not been located. Since RRC often had several literary irons in the fire at one time, this is not all that surprising.

RRC continued to lobby for a new edition of *Sky Determines* by the University of New Mexico. On February 4, 1965, he wrote Peter Hurd, who had illustrated the 1948 edition, "You and I are the ones most concerned in seeing the book is brought out again." (It was RRC, not Hurd particularly.) He backed this up by quoting the Highlands University librarian as saying he thought the book "should never [have been] permitted to go out of print." RRC added that Powell was becoming "most emphatic" about a new edition. Nothing indicates this was this case.

Chapter 8: Church Tensions

Within a year of the publication of *Sky Determines* RRC was at work on a new book. In his field notes of August 23, 1935, he jotted a note: "Today begins actual composition." He "dictated" four pages of chapter headings. I am puzzled by his use of "dictated." There is nothing to indicate RRC had a secretary. To whom could he have dictated his thoughts? Grace? Someone from the church? RRC's reply to the biography request from *American Men of Science* was on September 9, 1936. Dr. Moses provides an explanation why the second book shifted focus in "If There Be Sermons in Stone." He traces the evolution of RRC's various iterations of the focus of a second book and changes until finally the book appeared in 1946 as *River of the Sun: Stories of the Storied Gila*.

In a time when long distance calls were expensive and relatively rare and before the advent of email and other forms of social media, folks actually wrote letters. RRC and his bishop certainly did, on RRC's part sometimes two in one day. Sometimes their letters crossed in the mail. Some of the correspondence depicts RRC on the defensive about his pastoral duties, his parish expenditures, his building up of the church, relations with his flock, and most of all, how he spent his time. There is church correspondence in the Center for Southwest Research, but everything

I used for the book came from the Institute of Historical Survey Foundation. I concentrated on a series of sixteen letters from RRC beginning January 6, 1937, the tenth anniversary of his assumption of the ministry at the Church of the Good Shepherd, and running through October 2, 1940, just a month before Howden's death. To me, they seemed most typical and representative of dozens of other letters. During roughly the same period (March 18, 1937 to December 15, 1939) Bishop Howden wrote just eight; RRC out-wrote him two-to-one although the bishop had a secretary and RRC had none. RRC could get worked up; Howden was more solicitous and gentle. He could be insistent but was always civil. Throughout, their correspondence was always highly formal: however many times RRC saw Howden at diocesan gatherings, it was "Bishop Howden" and "Dr. Calvin," never first names.

RRC wrote Howden of the "long and persuasive" Phoenix letter raising the possibility of a new posting there on October 5, 1937. The letter seems to have signaled a shift in his relations with the bishop and marked the high water mark of his tenure at Good Shepherd. In the letter, RRC summarized the considerable gains and successes at Silver City while painting a much bleaker picture of the work at St. Luke's in Deming. Part of the problem was how many services were to be held there because of a loss in membership from fifty-two to thirty-two. If services were reduced, his $25 monthly stipend might be cut as well. Even so, RRC told Howden, he had told the St. Luke's parishioners that "as long as they will come, I will come, whether the stipend be paid or unpaid." He used another paragraph reminding Howden of his workload, although by then it appeared he was no longer ministering to the CCC. He suggested that all this might cause him to give the Phoenix situation "serious thought." That, of course, would force him "to abandon a ministry" that "reached far beyond the Good Shepherd." RRC had already reminded Howden that "with exceptional fatigue comes nervous exhaustion, and then very soon insomnia."

Bishop Howden appeared to apply the pressure in his letter of November 1, 1937, to "fish or cut bait" regarding RRC's possible move to Phoenix. There are several reasons for this: the state of health of both Calvins, the fact that Good Shepherd was not ready to become self-supporting and that meant more money problems, and the bishop's desire that more "general missionary work" be performed at Good Shepherd. All this, Howden concluded, "will make you feel warranted" to seriously consider the move. How much more "general missionary work" he expected RRC to perform is unspecified. RRC noted to Howden on November 2, 1937, that their letters had crossed in the mail, but he again defended himself about going to or spending any time in Phoenix, as had been alleged. He also told Howden that his accuser, a Rev. Moore, had never been in Silver City and, as a result, "what he could know about its prospects, I can hardly imagine." Moore had told Howden he thought he could build up Good Shepherd and make it self-supporting. That was good news to Howden of course.

RRC continued to try to clear up Howden's misconceptions. RRC said he knew the bishop "want(s) to be just to me." He also mentioned he had written no books or articles in 1937. Perhaps not, but he had three articles published in 1936 and another three in 1937, regardless of when they were written. Now, he saw a different picture in Deming; he wrote on November 2, 1937, that it looked as if things "had turned the corner" there, but noted that an increase in his expense account would allow him to spend an extra day working there.

RRC wrote about prisoners' reading matter September 22, 1937. Rank notwithstanding, Howden should have known better than try to get between RRC and his beloved incarcerated. Howden shot back with his "some cooperation needed" letter on September 29. "In Prison and You Visited Me Not" appeared in the April 1938 issue of *The Spirit of Missions*.

RRC had complained for years about the unreliability of his car, which he used for church business as well as personal transportation. Howden addressed the repair bill issue and RRC's "vague statement" about use of his car in a letter of April 4, 1937. Several months later, he unexpectedly sent a check, which RRC promptly used to buy a like-new second-hand 1936 Chevrolet. RRC thanked his bishop for making the trade-in possible.

While Pyle's comments about RRC come from *The New York World Telegram* of December 6, 1939, his columns were syndicated in dozens of newspapers, all of which probably used the article. RRC estimated forty. The Pyles and the Calvins apparently formed a warm bond in a short space of time during the newspaperman's visit in Silver City. A scrapbook of photos deposited by Peggy Balcolm with the Institute of Historical Survey Foundation contains the photograph of Pyle and his wife. Pyle (1900–1945) later became a war correspondent; he was killed by a Japanese sniper's bullet in the Okinawan prefecture of Ie Shima during the waning days of World War II.

Bishop Howden wrote RRC, March 18, 1937, that a fellow priest had complained of confused wording in the "Living Church" diocesan publication. RRC fired back immediately denying the allegation. The letter to Howden October 2, 1940, is marked LETTER NO. 2. October 5, 1937. It concerns RRC's "perplexity" with "Mrs. B." Letter No. 1 is missing, but RRC did imply in his October 2 letter that its subject was an expansion on the idea "Just now it is a difficult time here."

"Approach to the Temple of Science" appeared in his *Silver City Daily Press* column of July 21, 1938. "Fire in the Trees" appeared in *New Mexico Magazine*, July 1939.

Chapter 9: To the Plains: The Clovis Years

In his letter to J.C. Galbraith, December 29, 1942, expressing interest in the opening at St. Clement's in El Paso, RRC called his Silver City assignment "one of the obscurest posts in the Church."

The photograph accompanying many of RRC's articles in *Southwest Churchman* and elsewhere show him in a white clerical collar and rimless glasses, gazing intently into the camera's lens. He could be mistaken for a priest of the Church of England. One undated, unattributed article indeed called him "A High Churchman." After his ordination, RRC habitually wore the distinctive high collar that signified his profession. RRC told his grandchildren that he was "always a watcher" of the free and open sky. As his gaze turned downward, however, he began jotting down what he observed.

RRC's article on the new church building appeared in *New Mexico Magazine* for March 1950. The Right Reverend James M. Stoney DD wrote often of RRC and St. James in his memoir *Lighting the Candle* (Santa Fe: Rydall Press, 1961) but oddly not of its consecration. I could find nothing either by contacting St. James or the Clovis Public Library. Conversely, there does survive a handsome program depicting the groundbreaking ceremonies on Sunday, April 24, 1949. A photograph shows Bishop Stoney, RRC, and a host of church dignitaries and members watching Hilda Saunders turn the first shovel of earth. John Gaw Meem does not seem to be present. The program notes that Bishop Stoney had asked Ms. Saunders, a native of Rotherham, Yorkshire, England, to be the first to break ground because her "shoveling was symbolic of the strong ties" between St. James and "our beloved mother church" in England.

John Randall Calvin's comment as a source for his father "wreaking carnage" on Japanese merchant shipping comes from an email, February 19, 2015, concerning Rodney's service during World War II: "They [his squadron] worked mostly at night. He spoke of finding ships…with radar, dropping flares…then strafing and bombing them." John Randall noted that his father was only nineteen when he entered the Army Air Corps, and that "I can only imagine it was difficult for him, as the son of a priest, to use the triggers on his dual 50 caliber machine guns on the little Japanese kids his age...."

John Randall Calvin is the primary source (interview, October 10, 2013) of family anecdotal material on Margaret (Peggy) Calvin (1930-2006), later the Albuquerque socialite wife of businessman and politician Edward V. Balcolm. By all accounts, she was a beautiful woman. She certainly was as a child judging by her photos I have seen in family photo albums. I interviewed Edward V. (Ed) Balcomb (1923-2013) December 12, 2012 a year before his death in a busy Mexican restaurant (his chosen *comida*) in Belen, New Mexico, during a weekend lunch hour near where he was then living with his daughter, Dr. Teresa Balcolm. He was in failing health but managed to share several delightful stories of RRC's life in Clovis and Silver City.

Martha Choquette of Silver City shared her view of RRC in an interview with me on December 9, 2014.

Ross Jr.'s meetings with his father are described in an email from Charles, October 31, 2005, and an extract from a memoir Ross Jr. sent his son dated 07/01/2004. There had been times when RRC had not even acknowledged his son's existence. In an interview in 1934 with Lester Raines, for example, he had allowed Raines to assume he had just two children. RRC later wrote that he did not want to be reminded of Ross Jr.'s birth. Such pronouncements take on an Old Testament tone in which a father shuns a son and turns his back on him for perceived transgressions. The apparently final exchange of correspondence between RRC and Rodney in the late 1960s has much the same tenor.

Chapter 10: *River of the Sun:* The Gila

River of the Sun is totally unlike *Sky Determines*. I find the book to be much more readable, more attractive in appearance, and easier to get through. Like *Sky Determines* it attracted a slew of favorable reviews. Some of the more important ones were from *Arizona Monthly*, Vol. 22, November 1946; *Chicago Book Week*, April 14, 1946; *The Christian Century*, May 1, 1946; *Kirkus Review*, April 1, 1946 (Virginia Kirkus); *New York Herald Tribune Weekly Book Review*, May 5, 1946 (Erna Fergusson); *New York Times*, June 23, 1946 (John Weld); and *The Saturday Review*, June 8, 1946 (Stanley Vestal). Carl Hertzog (1902-1984) was as recognized in his field as RRC was in his. Josef Muench (1904-1998) was a Bavarian born photographer whose name, as one website puts it "became synonymous with *Arizona Highways*."

River of the Sun was dedicated to Grace Calvin. For the Lyons family reaction, see Ida F. Campbell and Alice F. Hill, *Triumph and Tragedy: A History of Thomas Lyons and the LCs* (Silver City, New Mexico: High- Lonesome Books, 2002).

An authority who put *River of the Sun* in context for me with other contemporary non-fiction works on the Southwest is my friend Bill Toth, who wrote me a long, thoughtful letter November 2014. Bill has written and spoken on Southwestern literature, is familiar with RRC, and knows of what he discourses.

Francis P. Farquhar published *The Books of the Colorado River and the Grand Canyon: A Selective Bibliography* (Los Angeles: Dawson, 1953). Lawrence Clark Powell reprinted his list as *A Southwestern Century: A Bibliography of One Hundred Books of Non Fiction about the Southwest* (Los Angeles: J. E. Reynolds, 1958).

RRC once approached Senator Barry Goldwater of Arizona for photos the senator might have taken of the Gila. The senator, a first-class photographer, responded warmly by mail on February 5, 1969, lamenting, "I wish I had been more attentive to this most important River [the Gila], but my first love is the Colorado."

Chapter 11: Later Publications

Thomas C. Donnelly put the project that led to "The People of New Mexico" into motion on August 16, 1946, suggesting RRC step outside his field to do a socio-political study of the people of the East and West sides of New Mexico. There is no indication Donnelly had ever met RRC or knew him except by reputation. He didn't even have Calvin's address, addressing his letter to "Dr. Ross Calvin, Episcopalian Rector, Clovis, New Mexico." Donnelly wrote RRC that his son, however, had seen him in the Jemez Mountains, "so I presume that as a plainsman [RRC had then been in Clovis four years] you were taking the opportunity to see the mountains." *River of the Sun* had just been published, and RRC's writing abilities must have been uppermost in Donnelly's mind. RRC accepted the commission to write the paper on September 11, 1946. Donnelly acknowledged receipt of the manuscript on February 22, 1947, saying, "Right off, I'll tell you that I like it personally," but he had no compunction in calling RRC's attention to what today would be his lack of "political correctness" in referring to the "Hispano" and their economic difficulties. (On August 16 Donnelly himself referred to Native Americans as "the Injun.") Following departmental protocol, Donnelly told RRC he would send the paper out for reading: "As soon as I have the advantage of their combined wisdom, I'll let you know of their weighty judgment." Except for how RRC referred to "Mexicans" and their economic plight, Donnelly found only relatively minor problems. The essay was published in *Population Trends in New Mexico* (Albuquerque: University of New Mexico Department of Government, Division of Research, 1947). There seems to be no information about how it was received.

Lieutenant Emory Reports: A Reprint of Lieutenant W. H. Emory's Notes of a Military Reconnoissance (Albuquerque: University of New Mexico Press, 1951) brought back a book that eminently deserves attention. The quotation about Emory's observational and botanical skills comes from L. G. Moses. RRC took pride in naming Emory Pass. He raised the issue in a "Village Parson" column in the *Silver City Daily Press* on July 12, 1938, and then announced in his column three days later that he himself had named it ("Emory Pass Now Named").

Three of RRC's books (*Sky Determines*, *River of the Sun*, and *Lieutenant Emory Reports*) enjoyed the prestige of reviews in *The New York Times*. The third review, by noted scholar J. Frank Dobie of *Lieutenant Emory Reports*, was on June 3, 1951. It was entitled "Boswell to the Open Prairie." RRC must have been pleased. Closer to home was another positive review by writer, historian, and old friend C. L. Sonnichsen in the *El Paso Herald-Post* on May 26, 1951.

"The Exotic Plants of New Mexico" appeared in *Mosaic of New Mexico's Scenery, Rocks, and History: A Brief Guide for Visitors*, edited by Paige W. Christiansen and Frank E. Kottlowski (Socorro, New Mexico: New Mexico Bureau of Mines and Mineral Resources, 1964).

The article on the Rev. Edward Lee Greene (1843–1915) appeared in the Autumn 1949 issue of *New Mexico Quarterly Review*. Jean W. Henderson wrote of Greene in *The Centennial History of the Church of the Good Shepherd* (Silver City, New Mexico: Unicorn Press, 1991).

RRC wrote Lawrence Clark Powell June 1, 1964, that John Van Dyke (1856–1932) most influenced his writing. Like Van Dyke, RRC loved the desert. He once said in an unpublished work called "Bright Panoramas" that he wanted to "track the desert down to its lair, to pursue it to the ocean's edge." Van Dyke's famous book *The Desert* was published in 1901. Richard Shelton, who provided an introduction to its reprint in the Peregrine Smith Literary Naturalists series (Salt Lake City: Peregrine Smith, 1980), called Van Dyke a "literary naturalist."

Clovis News-Journal of June 2, 1947, reported that Calvin was the author of two articles in the *See Your West* series. The second one, with Ansel Adams's photographs, appeared January 1, 1950. *New Mexico Magazine* articles included "River of the Sun," November 1945; "Church of the Apostles," February 1948; and the four-part "A Naturalist's Notebook," January 1953, February 1953, April 1961, February 1962.

Barnabas in Pittsburgh: From Common Clay to Legend (New York: Carlton Press, 1966) was self-published. RRC had only once before resorted to this method of getting his work in print (*A Mystical Bride*), although he did pay for half the publishing costs of *Sky Determines*. Carlton Press was a vanity press. The *Faith and Work* article on *Barnabas in Pittsburgh* appeared in the St. Barnabas journal Summer issue of 1966.

Chapter 12: Family Matters

The brief sketch "Thoughts in front of a crucifix on a 68th birthday" was handwritten on November 22, 1957. Just twenty-fives lines long, it is, after *A Mystical Bride*, the most personal of RRC's writings to survive and certainly the bleakest and the darkest. It is inconceivable why RRC permitted the paper to survive. This is the source of the quotation about "a son to me by blood is a stranger" and his fears about Grace's "incurable madness."

On December 30, 1955, RRC typed his brief comments marking his upcoming last full year at St. James. They were nostalgic and reflective but also requested help in making "this parish nearer what it ought to be—an outpost of the kingdom of God." He told his parishioners he looked forward to the "harvest years" in retirement so he could spend more time on study and writing. He explained that was because "most of my life has been spent in the pursuit of learning in one field or another."

RRC's announcement of his retirement at Clovis was a clear change from what had happened when he left Geneva. This time he wrote it himself instead of relying on a reporter to guess at what he was going to do next. The release was dated August 25, 1956, but was not published until January 1957. The editor printed it word-for-word. The article was headlined, "Dr. Calvin Retires from Parochial Ministry."

On October 24, 1960, Medical Administrative Assistant Albert E. Ball of the New Mexico State Hospital in Las Vegas wrote RRC to say that the medical staff was "in agreement" that Grace, "apart from the negative family history, which is the most significant finding in the case of Huntington's Chorea...did not present the symptoms of the disease." This somewhat confusing sentence clearly relieved RRC, especially when Ball told him there was "no basis for concern" for Rodney and Peggy.

The "black market" comment, as well as how RRC felt about Ross Jr's "blue collar roots," was shared by Charles in a March 2014 telephone interview. Charles sees this as another clash of world views that had much to do with his father's disappointment. The "organizing principle" statement from Ross Jr. was passed on to me by Charles on March 30, 2014. Charles says he knows of more than one such letter. That Ross Jr. would pull out the letter with the offensive language about his birthright every time he wanted to be reminded of his father's mistreatment must have been like running one's tongue over a sore tooth, but a thousand times worse. This was also the occasion for Charles's statement that his understanding of his father and grandfather's relationship came through "the lens" of his father's perception. It seems telling that Ross Jr.'s children always refer to their grandfather as "Doctor Calvin," never by any more familiar term.

RRC wrote Teresa regarding her grandmother Grace on March 21, 1962. RRC's thoughts about his own grandfather were contained in the same letter. RRC expressed his ideas about the value of education and religion to another granddaughter, Virginia, during the same time period. He had told the same thing to Teresa.

RRC wrote the Harvard admissions office April 21, 1965, urging grandson Charles's acceptance into the Class of 1969. He asked for a response "very soon, if you can." Charles told me of his reaction at not being accepted by Harvard in a December 14, 2014, email. He recalls being sanguine about being placed on Harvard's waiting list, saying he likely would not have applied "but for some sense of obligation [to his grandfather], or the supposed luminosity of the family."

RRC was always proud of the Calvin name and interested in the impression names make. He provided his advice to Rodney and Christine about naming their first child in a letter on March 5, 1953. They honored him by giving the baby RRC's middle name. John Randall clearly loved his grandfather. He shared his thoughts in an email to me on September 11, 2015, as the book was nearing completion and as he was heading back to the "Golden Eye" to resume his voyage around the world.

RRC seemed always to be concerned with money matters. He had frowned on Grace in Silver City for not keeping a tight enough rein on household expenses. John Randall believes his grandmother was "often emotionally beaten down" as a result of such episodes. He also feels Grace was "highly sensitive" and intelligent. According to Mary Calvin, a will on file for RRC in the Bernalillo County, New Mexico, Probate Court shows $87,657 was left after Ross Jr., attorneys, and final accounts were paid. Ross Jr. received $3500 of which he was instructed to spend

$500 for each of his children's education, leaving him $1000. The remainder was to be divided among Peggy and Rodney with five per cent to St. James Parish to establish a Grace Van D. Endowment for church maintenance. Rodney was named executor.

Mary Calvin believes the dispute between RRC and Rodney concerned the latter's impending divorce with Christine. He remarried, to Donna Justice, less than four months after RRC died.

Chapter 13: Cultivating His Garden

The delightful, albeit pensive, "Confessions of an Illegitimate Gardener" talk was given sometime in 1965. It is both entertaining and introspective at the same time. I rate it as perhaps my favorite of all RRC's essays for its tone and balance along with his ability to poke fun at himself, something he did not often do. RRC wrote again of his garden in the Autumn 1965 issue of *New Mexico Quarterly*. The garden, for him, in addition to being a physical place in which he found much-needed tranquility, was of course a strong metaphor for life.

Linda Shay, now an active member of Good Shepherd, as a girl had been taken by her parents from one Episcopal church to another around Albuquerque to attend services. She is the source of the comments on RRC's sermons there. John Randall gave his thoughts on his grandfather's sermons many times. Research aide Joshua Uffer found three of them in the Calvin Papers. "The Three Hours" was delivered Good Friday, April 4, 1958, at St. Mark's in Albuquerque and has seven sections. "Sainthood of the Upper Middle Class" was given February 16, 1964, at St. John's Cathedral in Albuquerque and repeated November 11, 1964, at St. Andrew's in Roswell.

The description of Iris Pearle Legg comes from an interview with John Randall (October 1, 2014). Mary Calvin subsequently offered more details in emails (February 12, 2015, and March 11, 2015).

In the Autumn 1965 essay for *New Mexico Quarterly* RRC wrote that his papers would have no readers and no one to write about them for a century or two following his death. L. G. Moses and I have proved him wrong.

One of RRC's goals for retirement, in addition to study and his garden, was travel. He took several trips with University of New Mexico groups to different European capitals. He wrote of one in a brief memoir that went through several iterations and titles before settling into something called "The Colors We Missed."

There is no indication it was ever published. The manuscripts are in Box 5, The Center for Southwest Research. Joshua Uffer (email, September 28, 2015) notes that the box also contains "Bright Panoramas," an incomplete memoir in which RRC compares himself to British diarist John Evelyn and discusses how his childhood pursuits led directly to the writing of *Sky Determines*.

The University of New Mexico conferred an honorary Doctor of Laws degree upon RRC at its June 4, 1953, commencement.

RRC's letter to the *Harvard Alumni Bulletin* was written May 22, 1969. He and a fellow alumnus, whose name I could not find, were outraged about faculty actions they clearly took strong objection to. It is RRC's only recorded admonishment of his beloved Harvard.

On January 7, 1966, Roland Dickey wrote from his University of New Mexico Press office to Lawrence Clark Powell about his concern for RRC's health and his apparent slipping memory. RRC alluded again to an episode with his health in a June 2, 1969, letter to a fellow Harvard alumnus. RRC believed he might have fallen victim to a stroke.

The letter to his grandchildren is undated, but RRC had wanted better relations with his family and to clear the air for some time. In a July 15, 1965, letter to Charles, RRC referenced a recent family get-together: "What a pity these contacts are so rare." He then told his grandson, "I wish you would come down to see me before long. (Charles then lived in Los Alamos with his family, his grandfather in Albuquerque.) There are old matters you should know about—matters as old as college days."

RRC's alleged railing against God and meeting death with "a curse on his lips" comes from Charles (email, December 29, 2014). We revisited the story in our interview in Santa Fe on September, 20, 2015. Charles reflected that the anecdote concerning the curse episode, "to the extent that it's true, must have come from Iris." He found it "hard to imagine" Rodney or Peggy as the source. He does not believe his father made up the story, "but the consistency of phraseology, and the satisfaction with which my father relayed it, may imply that he had put his own gloss on someone else's words, and made them more emphatic in the process." Charles said his father told the same story several times. RRC might have been rethinking his faith as far back as his "Thoughts in front of a crucifix on a 68th birthday," November 22, 1957.

The visit in Santa Fe with Charles followed one a month before in Las Cruces August 11 with Mary. While taking her son back to college in California she had stopped in Mesilla Park for research at the Institute for Historical Survey Foundation. They and my wife and I had dinner that evening where she added more to my understanding of family dynamics.

The gravestone reads: "Ross R. CALVIN 1889 † 1970." There is another large marker in the form of an Episcopal cross in the Brookston, Indiana, cemetery reading: "CALVIN: Ross Randall 1889–19__, and Adine Chilton 1890–1918."

www.ingramcontent.com/pod-product-compliance
Lightning Source LLC
Chambersburg PA
CBHW020053170426
43199CB00009B/265